Literature and Ethics
Essays Presented to A.E. Malloch

The essays in this volume honour Professor A.E. Malloch upon his retirement from the English Department of McGill University. Malloch's achievements as a nationally recognized spokesman on behalf of academic freedom and as a scholar and critic of equal ethical commitment are recognized by a group of colleagues, students, and fellow national advocates of just academic policies. The essays reflect Malloch's particularly ethical formulations of academic discourse, as they draw upon the topics of mental reservation, casuistry, rhetoric, confidentiality, and tenure as the condition of free discourse. But they honour him perhaps best of all in their union within this volume, which attempts an original definition of the relation between literature and ethics at a moment when the whole concept of ethical literary criticism is being widely reconsidered. This volume is not concerned with the study of ethical themes within literature. Instead, it asks what ethical conditions, in both the public and private spheres of social behaviour, are presupposed in literary communication between authors and readers. Answers are given in three broad categories. Part I examines literary conventions as forms of ethical indecision in studies of Empson, Hamlet, and Elizabethan portraiture. Part II defines the "ethics of the unsaid" as an act of resistance and judgment in the works of Austen, Irigaray, and Chaucer. And Part III considers discursive "networks," formally in Boethius, technologically in Joyce, and academically in the modern university's policies on tenure.

A.E. Malloch

Photo by Mary-Lynne Fiske

Literature and Ethics

ESSAYS PRESENTED TO A.E. MALLOCH

EDITED BY GARY WIHL AND

DAVID WILLIAMS

McGill-Queen's University Press
Kingston and Montreal

© McGill-Queen's University Press 1988
ISBN 0-7735-0662-4

Legal deposit second quarter 1988
Bibliothèque nationale du Québec

∞

Printed in Canada on acid-free paper

Canadian Cataloguing in Publication Data

Main entry under title
Literature and ethics : essays presented to
A.E. Malloch
Includes bibliographical references and index.
ISBN 0-7735-0662-4
1. Literature and morals.   2. Malloch,
A.E. (Archibald Edward), 1926-   .
I. Malloch, A.E. (Archibald Edward), 1926-   .
II. Wihl, Gary, 1953-   .   III. Williams,
David, 1939-   .
PN49.L48 1988   801'.3   C88-090089-x

Contents

Preface

The essays gathered for this volume constitute a partial recognition of the achievements of Archie Edward Malloch, who has chosen to withdraw from his academic career as a professor of English Literature in favour of devoting himself to volunteer pastoral work for his church. I say "partial" because there has been no attempt to make this volume a "full" recognition. How could it be? Academic work for Malloch has always been one dimension of a study of introspections (his Ph.D. thesis was on Donne's *Biathanatos*) and an elaborate discourse with others – students, colleagues, academic officers. What this volume is meant to present to Malloch and of Malloch is simply one part of that discourse as it is known by various academic friends.

The Festschrift is a peculiar genre, recognizable by its honouring of an individual scholar but otherwise undefined in scope or method. It is unusual to be in a position to match the individual with a closely linked set of academic topics, but such is the case with Archie Malloch. Ethics has always been one of Malloch's foremost concerns as a literary critic and as a teacher. He presents an example of the ethical critic at a time when ethics is central within the discipline of literary studies. "Literature and Ethics" – the phrase no longer suggests narrow thematic discussions of the character in a novel, or the tradition of didactic literature. The discipline has become too plural. To become a public interpreter of a literary text (the minimal definition of a professional teacher) one must adopt a stance towards the very concept of textuality, and this in turn involves notions of legitimacy and coherence. How does one share one's institutional, public space with other interpreters, students, colleagues, participants on a panel? For Malloch, these questions are ethical because in the pedagogy of texts authority and interpretive coherence originate in self-understanding and a respect for otherness. Perhaps two examples from Malloch's own work can help to define the ethical nature of literary communication.

In an essay exploring the term "architectonic" in Sir Philip Sidney's *Apologie*, Malloch writes: "Since the mode of proof in an oration is *cum suspicione*, we cannot expect to find doctrines set forth according to their own inner coherence. The orator's chief interest is in achieving a coherence that will unite his material and the particular audience he is addressing. In the best orations, however, it is possible to reconstruct the doctrine which the speaker has molded and disposed for his rhetorical purposes." I note the use of the word "best." All disputes, competing interpretations, and temperamental differences may reduce dialogue to the stratagems of rhetoric for some people. And there is no doubt that throughout his academic life Malloch saw the virtues of mental reservation, casuistry, and rhetorical modes of dispute, the "inner coherence" of what is often left unsaid. But the "best" rhetoric makes it possible to reconstruct intention and conscience, not so much for the sake of establishing a definitive "truth" as to keep the focus of the analysis on its ethical purpose. For Malloch, the "architectonic" consists in self-knowledge, but that does not make it a "private and individual affair." The bearing of such knowledge is "primarily ethical and political." That is because rhetoric, cognition, and self cannot be dissociated, though they may often appear to function incoherently if one aspect is examined in isolation from the others. Ethics in its academic context teaches this lesson, regardless of what academics teach about ethical themes in any given text or departmental course. Ethics in literary criticism is a matter of defining the limits, reserves (in the double sense of untapped knowledge and knowledge that is deliberately withheld), and structures of a discourse; and not every teacher will want to participate in this "game" (I use the word seriously) of definition.

The second example I draw from Malloch's "A Dialogue on Plagiarism," written in 1976. The form of the essay already says much about the author, though the choice of topic perhaps even more. Many teachers have a policy about student plagiarism, but few (Neil Hertz is one who comes to mind) have thought the concept of plagiarism through to its implications for pedagogical discourse as a whole. On the surface the issue seems by definition "ethical," a matter of dishonesty and theft deserving punishment from academic authorities. But Malloch turns the issue upside down, making it a symptom of a structural problem within the academic community. Students plagiarize not to save themselves work (often a plagiarized essay spends as much work covering up its sources as its "innocent" counterpart spends revealing them). No, plagiarism signifies the way in which pedagogy that distances selves or objectifies standards of evaluation invites students to opt out of a dialogue with their teachers and with other students. Plagiarism might be seen as a "lie," hiding one's self under the words of another; but more likely it is an act of withdrawal, indicative of a general impoverishment of discourse. The question finally becomes: how do we reconcile the ideal of a close relation between student and instructor with the need to employ standards of objectivity and impartiality? That is the question which plagiarism, a supposedly easy case of applying standards, opens for consideration. Malloch's answer:

I'm not arguing that the relation between instructor and student is merely personal. I'm not even sure there is such a thing as a "merely" personal relation. Being a person at all, as the origin of the word implies, means exercising our being within a given role. Being an instructor or student means taking on roles that may overlap, but don't coincide with, our familiar or domestic roles, and it means accepting distinct responsibilities and restraints. If you want to call a conscientious playing of the instructor role "objectivity," fine, but let's not be baffled by our own metaphors, especially when they're derived from rather creaky epistemology. You hear "objectivity" talked about as though it were something we achieve simply by refraining from being "subjective." In fact, there isn't anything we think or say or do that isn't "subject" within the person we are.

Again, self, cognition, and rhetoric (or epistemology and metaphor) are all linked ethically, but no particular doctrine or value is asserted as a specific reform or guideline for a benevolent system of correction. What matters is the dialogue itself, which will define its own limits, since the knowledge of a text, or the rhetorical shaping of that knowledge, must be eventually exchanged with another.

Malloch's work may be divided into three broad categories, each reflected in the structure of this volume. His early studies in Renaissance rhetoric, paradox, and sensibility puzzle over the limits of self-expression within highly conventionalized modes of discourse. The essay on Sidney perhaps typifies this early work in its assumption of a coherent self that communicates with an audience by means of rhetorical devices. Malloch's subsequent work on Donne and casuistry, mental reservation, equivocation, and his increasing interest in novelists such as Jane Austen seem to mark a shift in thinking toward the ethics of the

unsaid. Silence, internal "speech," and hidden intentions all may become means of resisting abusive authority or of maintaining ethical
consistency. For the past fifteen years, Malloch has written less as a
scholar than as a politician concerned with questions of academic policy, confidentiality, freedom of expression, liberalization of curriculum,
and the like. There is a progression from one stage to the next. The
lessons of each stage are ethical and so too is the lesson of this volume,
its inner coherence inspired by each contributor's essay as a response
to Malloch. Such a dialogue should in principle be infinitely extendable,
so that the volume does less in the way of "monumentalizing" Malloch
as a person or a scholar and more in the way of setting before the
academic audience some of his linked ethical concerns as they bear on a
set of wide literary and pedagogical interests.

Part I, "Forms of Indecision," treats the problematic nature of self-
expression as it hovers between the ideal of transcending conventions
of utterance and extreme self-limitation. The three essays in this part
confine their treatment of the topic to the late Elizabethan and early
Caroline periods. I present a theoretical problem in William Empson's
concept of poetic ambiguity, which can mean either a richness of expression of great social value to various speakers or a multiplicity of
meanings so profuse as to be irrational and private. Empson focused his
typology of ambiguity on Elizabethan and Metaphysical poets. Dean
Frye chooses to focus on Hamlet, perhaps the Elizabethan type of
indecision. Hamlet shows a frustration with the necessities of convention, even as the play alludes to the Elizabethan scepticism about rational behaviour outside the norms of custom and forbearance. Hamlet
presents the problematical relation between self and action that is both
fascinatingly concentrated in its behaviour yet by this very concentration also a "radical simplification," a stagy Elizabethan character-part.
Leslie Duer treats another aspect of this problem within the same historical period in the shifting conventions by which a person's life is
summarized after death. His essay places Shakespeare himself within
the problem, as he compares his representative Elizabethan tomb
sculpture, with all its conventionality and surface coding, with the
emergent "mimetic" or "realistic" tomb sculpture soon to replace it.
Paradoxically, greater fidelity to "lifelike" representation leads to a loss
of coherent signification. An aesthetic tension emerges between the
refined compositional techniques of Dutch portraiture and the lack of
directional guidance it offers to the viewer used to the emblematic
codes of the extant monumental surfaces.

Part II, the "Ethics of the Unsaid," contains three essays that are chronologically separate yet remarkably connected in the topic they treat. Elaine Bander makes an original and important contribution to Austen studies and the study of the novel by distinguishing between interior dialogue, indirect discourse, and *narratorial silence*, not to be confused with authorial silence. Austen displays a mode of judging self-awareness and everyday levels of sympathetic understanding in her use of reflective silences within her novels. Silence, an easily overlooked element in speech rhythms, is shown to be on a par with the elements usually associated with Austen: narrative wit and lively dialogue. Silence has a way of circumventing the conventions of restricted speech and is also linked to the responsibilities of holding secrets and accepting confidences. Austen's silent women exceed the limits of imposed silence favoured by patriarchal moralists. The topic leads directly to Maggie Berg's treatment of Luce Irigaray, and the general problem of an authentic female voice within a culture dominated by the values of a male-centred language. She attempts to defend Irigaray's non-binary approach to verbal meaning, meaning as neither strictly masculine nor feminine, neither controlled nor unconscious, by focusing on Irigaray's use of boundaries, margins, and the physicality of lips – all means of defining, without fixing, the difference between speech's exhibiting of one truth while withholding another, secret, one. There is always a hidden remainder in speech, but it is not to be dismissed, especially in women, as passivity or "unconscious" inferiority. Finally, David Williams treats the philosophical implications of the unsaid in Chaucer's the Friar's Tale, and attempts to connect neo-Platonic doctrines of intentionality with contemporary speech-act theory. For Williams, as for the two other contributors within this section, discourse proves to be as much a matter of what is unsaid as what is said. The act of communication in Chaucer's fiction is part of dialectical process that retracts certain authorial intentions even as it heuristically opens the discovery of truths.

The last section, "Networks," presents aspects of social discourse at the broadest level of concern within literature and the academic community. Abbott Conway returns to the medieval trivium and quadrivium in order to find a rational model for a curriculum devoted to ethical and intellectual self-improvement. His discussion presents an interesting example of the fullness of formal reasoning, especially as it touches on concerns in the other essays. His discussion of the ethico-rational analysis of the centre and the periphery presents a vision of tyranny and anarchy as timely as that of another well-known trivial/quadrivial thinker, James Joyce. Donald Theall, a Joyce expert and, like Malloch, a former student of Marshall McLuhan, treats Joyce's response to the massive effects of technology on all social intercourse. For Theall, Joyce is a Socialist-Anarchist, who follows Marx in seeing technologies as reshaping the sensorium, and redefining the very concept of what it is to be human. Joyce anarchistically celebrates discontinuities, "transverse dimensions" of communication, as Proust and Gilles Deleuze do, but the impulse behind the celebration remains Utopian and firmly committed to human improvement. The book as machine mixes pluralist anarchy with ordered chaos.

Finally, David Braybrooke, one of North America's leading moral philosophers, tells us somewhat ironically that he is offering a "modest" defence of the concept of tenure against its free-market critics who advocate a university system of renewable contracts. This issue is likely to be of the utmost practical and ethical concern to readers of this volume. His essay refers several times to Malloch's own work in defence of the tenure system, particularly in its "deep" or underlying arguments, which are not about costs and benefits but about the whole concept of collegial discourse within an academic community. It is in the elaborate definition of discourse and freedom that two old friends, Malloch and Braybrooke, meet and involve us all. I place Braybrooke's essay last as complementary to my own on Empson, since Braybrooke takes the opportunity to work out some further details of his theoretical model of how decision making proceeds in the face of uncertainty. There is an interesting parallel here to Empson's literary-utilitarian effort to measure the social applications of the most strained poetic ambiguities, what he calls structures of "indecision."

The publication of this volume would not have been possible without the support and assistance of several people. Leanore Lieblein played an important advisory role in the early stages of the volume's preparation. Valentina Matsangos helped in ways too numerous to list. Robert Holton provided technical assistance and prepared the index. Richard Salisbury, Dean of McGill's Faculty of Arts, encouraged the preparation of this book from the outset and acted on behalf of Malloch's students over the past thirty years in supporting its publication.

Gary Wihl

Archibald Edward Malloch
vir bonus dicendi peritus

As a member of the English Department at McGill University and (earlier) at Toronto, Carleton, and Western, Archie Malloch has been a member of the Canadian academic community for almost four decades. His extraordinary contribution to that community arises out of his philosophy of community itself – as a lived experience shared with others with an unusual degree of generosity and sensitivity.

As a teacher he has regarded students not as clients of a professional practice or as customers in some educational market, but as younger members of a collegium participating in a common pursuit of knowledge. Largely owing to his influence the rapport between staff and students in English at McGill is exceptional: he has helped students and colleagues to grow intellectually, personally, and socially.

Archie contributed clarity of thought to the governmental structures of McGill University, especially its Senate. His was the rare quality not only of reading, but also of understanding and remembering the reams of documents produced by Senate over the years. He became a living source of reference for those wishing to know the history of a question. In Senate his arguments were always to the written fact, and always informed by reason. He showed neither fear nor favour towards those in authority, though his rigour was tempered by a witty turn of phrase. All his effort was bent towards calling Senate back to basic principles. In many ways he has been like the University's conscience.

Not only did he reshape English studies at McGill; he contributed to the academic community at large in Canada. Archie grew to be one of Canada's foremost authorities on academic freedom, respected by all for his wisdom and probity. He was Chairman of the Academic Freedom and Tenure Committee of the Canadian Association of University

Teachers from 1970 to 1974, and was responsible as well for a number of CAUT investigations from one end of the country to the other. In 1979 CAUT honoured him with the Milner Memorial Award, which is given only occasionally, and only for outstanding contributions to the cause of academic freedom. He is noted for his careful, deliberate, and judicious way of approaching problems, seeking the essence of them, and finding just and workable solutions. But his analytic ability and skill in constructing the just solution have their beginning not in relation to the abstract "problem," but in his sensitivity to the human person with a problem. In any list of Archie Malloch's many virtues and talents, the origin of them all would be found in his compassion.

As a scholar he has written significant papers on such topics as the Renaissance paradox, casuistry (in John Donne), the definition of sin, the habit of forbearance (in Jane Austen), equivocation, mental reservation (in the recusants), McLuhan's discourse, confidentiality, plagiarism, tenure, peer evaluation, academic freedom (and its limits), papers which are all of a piece with the man Archie Malloch because they are all about the possibility of knowledge and the problems of its communication and exchange among members of the educated human community. Despite the importuning of colleagues, he has always shunned high administrative office, preferring the role of counsellor and adviser. A man of commitment makes choices, and Archie's have been for the human and communal first, for the shared life of knowledge and experience, before the narrow, the abstract, the cerebral. For him research is not meant to be a secret code but an open scholarship interacting directly with teaching.

Archie's life has been closely tied to medicine through immediate forebears who were connected to Sir William Osler.* His grandfather, A.E. Malloch (1844–1919), was a physician-colleague and close friend of Sir William's. His father, T.A. Malloch (1887–1953), was Sir William's disciple, an attending physician during his last illness, the widowed Lady Osler's surrogate son, counsellor, and correspondent, coeditor of the large *Bibliotheca Osleriana* (1929), and has been acknowledged as one of the great modern physician-librarians. Moreover, his mother Kitty (K.E.E.A. Malloch, 1899–1982) was Sir William's grandniece. Archie has thus been aware from the beginning of medicine as, among other things, a science of personal relations with a long and venerable,

*For the Mallochs' relations with the Oslers, see Frederick B. Wagner, *The Twilight Years of Lady Osler: Letters of a Doctor's Wife* (Canton, MA: Science History Publications, 1985).

learned history. As a member of the Board of Curators of the Osler Library at McGill he has nurtured Osler's humanistic philosophy of medicine as an interdisciplinary humane science. For several years, at the Montreal Convalescent Hospital, he has carried his warmth and counsel into the Palliative Care Unit, working with patients and their families. Presently he is continuing his work as a volunteer in bereavement counselling at the Royal Victoria Hospital.

His pre-university education at Kent School, Connecticut, gave him the early, formative experience of community through education with a committed, Christian basis of lived, communal experience. The concepts of "community" and "communication" define Archie Malloch's university career as much as his career has been devoted to helping to define and enrich that community. The community of Archie Malloch has been much wider than the university, the university being but a microcosm of the larger human commonwealth. In addition to his hospital work, he has for some time been instructing in the reading of Scripture in his downtown Anglican parish. Archie exercises the same care and concern in the greater human community as he does in the smaller, the family. His devotion to his own family has been the source of his ethical commitment to the institutions of society, such as the Church, the university, medicine, and governance.

No book can capture all of Archie's many lively interests or represent his several exemplary commitments. In this collection of essays, initiated and sponsored by members of the English Department at McGill, to honour him upon his retirement from the university, members of the Canadian academic community attempt to respond to a colleague who has contributed outstandingly to that community. Colleagues across the country wish him present and future happiness in his endeavours scholarly, consultative, arbitrative, ethical, and religious.

Alan Heuser

Literature and Ethics

Empson's Generalized Ambiguities

Unlike most contemporary theorists his equal in sophistication, the late Sir William Empson appeared to be remarkably free of doubt. He was always happy to apologize for the clumsiness of some of his critical methods: any paraphrase or interpretive scheme, he suggests as early as *Seven Types of Ambiguity* (1930), lags well behind the immediate, intuitive grasp of the poem's verbal tensions, what he called the "forces" essential to a poem's "totality." But the analytically simplified presentation of these forces does not exclude semantic precision or, more important, a measurable degree of usefulness. Even more than his mentor I.A. Richards, Empson considered the attentive reading of poetry as a device or "machine" for modifying egocentric habits and developing moral attitudes. Most of the time Empson's studies of the phases of poetic ambiguity, the social contradictions within the pastoral genre, and the semantic "equations" of opposed meanings (what he called "complex words") is mistaken for a pre-New Critical elaboration and defence of a unique, literary aspect of language, its special "manysidedness" (Cleanth Brooks).[1] But such an emphasis necessarily downplays the pragmatic dimension of Empson's work, his effort to explain semantic contradictions as the consequence of one speaker's use of a term colliding with another's until a small scale consensus is reached.[2] Beneath Empson's apparently technical analysis of grammar, tropes, and polysemy, there lies a special confidence that the pragmatic function of language is never in danger of confusion or error. Wherever he discovers the possibility of divergent, even contradictory, readings of a poem, play, or novel, he also finds a proportionally greater effort to establish a normative discourse, or with complex words, an ideology.

Empson's faith in the pragmatic function of language seems to place him close to speech-act theorists, such as J.L. Austin and John Searle, and at a distance from his most recent deconstructionist admirers, J. Hillis Miller and the late Paul de Man – critics with their own special interest in antithetically structured meanings. De Man used to speak of Empson as this century's greatest English critic, but this admiration seems tendentious when we connect it with de Man's early review essay on *Seven Types of Ambiguity* and *Some Versions of Pastoral* (1935).[3] De Man speaks of the implicit crisis in Empson's work, his profound sense of "limitless anteriority" in poetic ambiguity which defeats all definite understanding and all "utilitarian" efforts to organize the individual's appetencies and impulses in the manner of Richards's speculative psychology of reading. De Man looks to Empson as an "ontological" critic, perhaps so that he may separate Empson from the naive equation of word and impulse he finds in Richards's literary criticism.

Christopher Norris, before he began a series of books on deconstruction, offered the first (and so far only) detailed theoretical study of Empson.[4] One of his recent essays offers, I think, the fairest account of de Man's limited affinity with Empson. Norris suggests that in one dimension Empson has much more in common with de Man than with, for example, Brooks, because Empson insists that verbal ambiguities present genuine conceptual problems and define socially acceptable bounds of rationality; ambiguities are not to be confused with poetic fancies, nor is there any aesthetic satisfaction to be gained from paradox or irony.[5] Empson and de Man part company at the point where de Man would impose a "rhetoric of crisis," an "essential" estrangement of consciousness within the poetic. Empson always comes back to some stronger version of rational agreement on the far side of the (provisional) mental disorientation of ambiguity. In the end the pragmatic Empson seems to cancel the proto-deconstructionist Empson. But perhaps it is only an illusion of cancellation.

I agree with Norris's careful distinctions, but I can well imagine another essay entitled, after Norris and Empson himself, "Some Versions of Consensus," comparing Empson with Stanley Fish instead. In this essay the Empson interested in logical disorder might appear the stronger version when set in relief against a pragmatic critic who argues strenuously for the socially prescribed rules for accepting or rejecting an ambiguity, or with a critic who would see ambiguity itself as imposed or worked up in a text by those readers determined (by their belief in its magical value) to find it there in the first place. The apparent ease with which Empson can be fitted, at least provisionally, into a variety of critical contexts is itself an example of Empsonian ambiguity.

But we cannot leave Empsonian ambiguity happily there, for it is not the same as relativism or pluralism, not for Empson and not for any of the other critics with whom he might be compared. Empsonian ambiguity forces connections between opposites; it does not permit us to rest content with an inert pluralist mix. The ambiguity of Empson's critical position is our own shared predicament. Brooks cannot assimilate Empson to New Criticism, but neither can de Man assimilate him to deconstruction. And Stanley Fish, another overt admirer of Empson, has trouble assimilating him to the interpretive community, again because he must eliminate ambiguity and contradiction from language in order to maintain that it is the informed reader's beliefs and intentions that put it there in the first place.

It probably matters very little which camp claims Empson. The usefulness of these tentative alignments is the way they bring into focus larger theoretical and ethical problems. In the rest of this essay I present a very select series of increasingly difficult examples of poetic ambiguity (following Empson's own ranking of their difficulty). In them we may see Empson trying to reconcile a plausible social situation with the logical contradictions of a poem's language. The technical and rhetorical refinement with which contradictions are unpacked seems to call into question rather than confirm pragmatic, ethical consensus. Specifically, I discuss examples of what Empson calls "generalized" ambiguity because these, as Norris first noted, are his crucial instances of "linguistic sanity and normative usage."[6] The point at which an ambiguity becomes generalizable is, for Empson, the point at which it fulfills its pragmatic function of establishing, however vaguely and non-formally, a stable agreement between speakers or between readers and poets; intentions are realized and beliefs strengthened. My examples, not surprisingly, tend to focus on Metaphysical Poets such as George Herbert or Richard Crashaw, because, as A.E. Malloch has noted, Empson saw in the Metaphysicals how "the dual applications of a word or phrase set up relations between themselves which are analogous to the relation between speakers in a dialogue."[7]

Empson on the "feeling of generalization" or "the background of human experience" that emerges from the consideration of a set of verbal contradictions sounds a lot like Austin on the basic vagueness of most practical linguistic conventions, or like Stanley Fish on the inability to formalize the ways in which people reach agreement all the time.[8] But of course a deconstructionist would not be so happy with this approach, seeing in a non-determinable background of meanings no easy possibility of a transition to a discussion of situation, intention,

social rules, and the like. The deconstructionist looks upon the pragmatist's faith in basic intelligibility as an evasion, a resort to the indefinite
as a means of covering contradiction.[9] Empson's feeling of generalization forces us to consider these two radically opposed views together.

From the opening pages of *Seven Types* Empson makes clear that "ambiguity" should be understood as a shorthand term for a poem's pragmatic context. Ambiguity is not a verbal device, related to wit or subtle-
ty of implication, but the "context implied by the statement, the person
to whom it seems to be addressed, and the purpose for which it seems
to be addressed to him."[10] Even Empson's harshest critics have acknowledged that he is never interested in verbal puzzles but always in
some situation that would justify the possibility of multiple meanings.[11]
Empson's treatment of ambiguity has very little in common with standard linguistic definitions. He does not waste effort sorting out homo-
nyms or syntax as if they were semantic flaws; he is interested in them
only insofar as they bear on special contexts of speaking. He even
suggests that his sort of ambiguity is impeded by verbal fuzziness.
Semantic meaning should be clear and then it may become ambiguous
as it calls upon sources of conflict in the beliefs of various speakers.
    How does generalization qualify the importance of some of these
ambiguities? Generalization becomes Empson's utility principle: When
an ambiguity may be generally extended to include whole classes of like
situations, it elevates verbal tension above merely "ornamental" comparisons of things' qualities and properties. In *Seven Types* generalizations occupy a crucial if difficult-to-define zone. They make possible the
transition from relatively simple ambiguities (multiple meanings that
do not necessarily cause any psychological tension) to the most complex ones (the overlap of distinct experiential categories to the point of
apparent irrationality). These degrees of ambiguity are outlined at the
outset by Empson, and the question of each degree's general relevance
to multiple contexts is gradually introduced as we move toward the
more complex types. The intensity of an ambiguity depends on the
force with which multiple meanings are joined: "Thus a word may have
several distinct meanings; several meanings connected with one another; several meanings which need one another to complete their
meaning; or several meanings which unite together so that the word
means one relation or one process" (5). A set of parallel psychological
states is offered, ranging, in reverse order, from "an indecision as to
what you mean" to "an intention to mean several things" down to a
"probability that one or other or both of two things has been meant,

and the fact that a statement has several meanings." The seven types are a refinement upon this scale.

In the simple stage of ambiguity, where the force pushing together different meanings is minimal, generalization is invoked very casually or not at all, as in this example of a Type I:

> Beauty is but a flower
> Which wrinkles will devour.
> Brightness falls from the air.
> Queens have died young and fair.
> Dust hath closed Helen's eye.
> I am sick, I must die.
>   Lord, have mercy upon us.

(Nashe, *Summer's Last Will and Testament* in Empson, 25)

The third line has two possible meanings. Either Helen's beauty has faded in the same way that the bright sun or moon fades daily behind the horizon (suggesting an elegiac mood), or the falling brightness refers to the dust of line 5, the motes in the air. This dust is generated by Helen's corruption. Is the falling brightness dirty and infectious? or is it merely the lightness and gaiety of humanity (especially in summer) which shall turn to dust in the grave? The brightness is vague in meaning; it applies easily to either reading and so sets up a pleasant or witty choice of readings. All that matters for Empson in this example is the possibility of the choice. We are not forced to consider corruption *as if it were* gay, or the reverse. The effect of the line is nugatory and so it easily yields to a vague, inclusive mood that could be called generalization about the human condition. In discussing Type I ambiguities, Empson uses the term "generalization" to speak of a sense of detachment, a cool view of human vanity in the face of death, as in an analogous example from Synge on page 41. There is no difficult tension that demands resolution.

Empson is off to a good pragmatic start. I suppose he prefers to emphasize the ambiguous rather than the generalizable, the contradictory rather than the peacefully resolved, because he wants to present the multiplicity of meanings in a poem which may not be obvious to readers conditioned to look down upon ambiguity. Hence the familiar (if misguided) charge that he is mostly interested in displaying his own ingenuity. Conflicts and tensions do not emerge fully until we arrive at Type III ambiguities, in which there is an attempt to unite, not merely display, distinct meanings. Sometimes the union of distinct meanings seems to be compelling; it may come close to political allegory and other risky methods of evading censorship under volatile and competitive circumstances; or it may seem vacuous and insignificant. Generalizations in this context of multiple relevance introduce an element of uncertainty into the purported resolution. They begin to approach what will become, later, the "structure of indecision." In feeling the pressure within a poem to connect logically distinct classes of objects or people, is our overall sense of the poem's relevance diminished or enhanced? And if enhanced, does this necessarily imply some normalizing function, some resolution of conflict? We may be able to give full recognition to a poem's insistence on comparing unlike things yet find that its pragmatic purpose remains unclear. Empson writes:

An ambiguity of the third type, then, as a matter concerning whole states of mind, occurs when what is said is valid in, refers to, several different topics, several universes of discourse, several modes of judgment or of feeling. One might call this a general ambiguity of the third type; ... Now, there are two main ways of constructing such an ambiguity. It may make a single statement and imply various situations to which it is relevant; thus I should call it an ambiguity of this type when an allegory is felt to have many levels of interpretation; or it may describe two situations and leave the reader to infer various things which can be said about both of them; thus I should call it an ambiguity of this type when an ornamental comparison is not merely using one thing to illustrate another, but is interested in two things at once, and is making them illustrate one another mutually.   (111–12)

The first sort of generality, termed "allegory," has a meaningful structure that remains constant on one level of interpretation. Its generality has to do with its being relevant under a wide variety of circumstances. It is close to what Empson calls a "proposition," some widely shared, common experience. The second sort is a little trickier because the resolution of the two different situations is achieved by mutual comparison; each side of the comparison claims equal importance. It anticipates what will become Empson's working definition of the pastoral. Strangely, however, mutual comparisons inhibit our sense of their overall relevance. They share a rhetorical structure similar to allegory but they do not seem widely applicable. In fact their function may be the evasion of contradictions – psychological and social – so that their generality hides a false consciousness. Mutual comparison may be seen in Shakespeare's description of an orderly state as a hive of honeybees:

> for so work the honey-bees
>
> ...
>
> They have a king, and officers of sorts;
>
> ...
>
> Others like soldiers, armed in their stings,
> Make boot upon the summer's velvet buds;
> Which pillage they with merry march bring home,
> To the tent-royal of their emperor;
> Who, busied in his majesty, surveys
> The singing masons building roofs of gold;
> The civil citizens kneading up the honey.

(*Henry V*, Act 1, Scene 2; Empson, 112)

The elevation of both parties is accomplished: "matters are so arranged that the only things the reader thinks of as in common between men and bees are the more tolerable things about either of them." The pain of labour is transformed into merry, song-like buzzing; everyone finds joy in building a lavish palatial structure. But this generalized meaning serves only one purpose: the cancellation of social conflict. The generosity of feeling which the verse is supposed to evoke hides violence and suffering, and so it does not really extend one's insight into social norms; it sets up a false norm. Here we might prefer more ambiguity, a finer sense of the incompatibility between the terms of the comparison instead of a generalization, even if this were at the expense of the poetry's normative claims.

I should emphasize that Empson does not hold up this mutual comparison as a poetic ideal. He is deeply interested in the way incompatible classes are fitted together. The danger lies in confusing a nonce generalization, as in *Henry V*, with the much greater pragmatic impulse to make verse as generally relevant as possible, to treat it as an allegory. Empson resists this impulse, but only on the grounds of *rhetorical undecidability*, and here he seems to have more in common with the deconstructionist reader. Because mutual comparisons are often indistinguishable from allegories (in which one side of the comparison dominates), Empson is cautious about making any sweeping claims for a particular poem's value. He is able to detect in the comparison of the bees with society a call for sympathy or generosity of feeling, but he does not invest it with great significance; indeed, he finds it to be "limited." But as soon as there is a lessening of the poem's ambiguity, its refusal to cohere into one (perhaps unnamed) meaning, which is its only resistance to generalization, the tendency to read it as a stabilizing, normative context for discussion grows considerably, and here Empson seems to have more in common with the pragmatic reader. Allegory and mutual comparisons turn up frequently as important tropes throughout Empson's writings, often with the purpose of establishing social norms. They seem to involve a great deal of risk, however. They seem to make Empson's pragmatic solutions to an ambiguous "case at hand" shift unpredictably to a higher level of generalization in order to solve massive, large-scale sorts of conflict. [12] Similarly, ambiguity shifts from being a flexible, responsive attitude to a mere semantic obstacle that should be overcome quickly so that we may get on happily with the development of our everyday habits.

The sort of danger I am outlining may be seen in another crucial example of generalized ambiguity, an "allegorical" stanza from Herbert's *The Temple* :

I gave to Hope a watch of mine: but he
    An anchor gave to me.
Then an old prayer-book I did present:
    And he an optick sent.
With that I gave a viall full of tears:
    But he a few green eares:
Ah, Loyterer! I'le no more, nor more I'le bring.
    I did expect a ring.   (Empson, 118)

Here the undecidability of the verse's overall structure is felt more acutely. Because the language is flat and uses elementary symbols, there is a temptation to read it as a simple allegory. It seems to invite a playful testing of various interpretive possibilities. Is the anchor the hope of resurrection or simply the power of holding out for a change in the lover's attitude? Is the prayer-book a symbol of an ordered, temperate life or the book that sanctifies the marriage ceremony? Is the vial of tears a mark of repentance or of the pain of sensual denial? And so on. To the degree that these alternate interpretations do not ask to be compared directly, or equated, the poem is strictly ambiguous. In fact Empson suggests a third possible interpretation. Perhaps the poem is about secular ambition "since the notion of exchanging presents suggests Court ceremonial and modes of obtaining preferment, and the *ring* might be a mark of office" (120). At the same time, the flatness of the symbols invites an allegorical generalization: "It may be read so as to convey, apparently in terms of the imagined movements of muscles, a statement of the stages of, a mode of feeling about, *any* prolonged endeavour; so that the reader is made to accept them all as alike in these particulars, and draw for his sympathy on any experience of the kind he may have had." The symbols become "musical," devoid of any particular set of referents. This would cancel completely any trace of ambiguity in the poem's meaning, for Empson continues, it is "absurd" to call a generalization "ambiguous because it has several particular cases." In sum: "In so far as a generalisation is thought of as the aggregate of the particular cases which have been chosen to test it, it may be called an ambiguity: in so far as, accepting it, you regard the taking of particular cases as a use of it rather than as an unpacking of its meaning, it becomes a single proposition" (121).

The Herbert poem makes possible an easy shifting back and forth between ambiguity and generalization. The close reader, paying attention to the poem's ambiguous symbols, will surely come up with antithetical interpretations which remain unresolved. The task of interpretation becomes the establishment of a primary meaning, marriage or redemption; but this meaning remains unstable. The pragmatic reader, recognizing the "hopelessness" of a definitive interpretation, allows the symbols to be used as a simple generalization, a statement that could apply to an infinite number of situations involving patience. The pragmatic reader finds sameness and repetition in the everyday world; the reader interested in ambiguity finds conflicting needs of totally distinct orders of experience. Which reading, the ambiguous or the pragmatic, has the greater value, and which is the more normative? Conflict or sympathetic identification?

Empson's overall argument makes it appear likely that the ambiguous reading is to be preferred. *Seven Types* moves through stages of increasingly deeper social and psychological conflict. In the generalized comparison of bees and the state the generalization served a narrow, temporary purpose and seemed to verge on the "ornamental." In Herbert's poem, however, generalization is seen as a way out of a very serious impasse. Herbert's symbols, far from providing resistance to an over-pragmatic explanation, seem to invite and sustain it. Is this a lapse in Empson's argument? or does it reveal a tendency to over-normalize conflicting readings? In the early stages of *Seven Types* generalization is rarely invoked, but then the early stages of ambiguity do not represent sharp mental conflicts. It now seems that Empson is beginning to push too far the evasion of certain indeterminate meanings. In many situations, especially those which speech-act philosophers like to focus upon (taking vows and getting married), the pragmatic approach is the sensible one. But when it is used to evade or flatten a certain rhetorical complexity (deciding whether or not something is meant to be taken allegorically), then the normative cannot be said to differ from the aberrant. A final example should make this clear.

In the chapter on the seventh and most conflicting sort of ambiguity Empson faces his greatest interpretive challenges. Crashaw is the exemplary case. Like Herbert, Crashaw writes a poetry that invites two interpretations, one sexual, the other religious. The combination is so strained that Empson thinks Crashaw would have been fit for psychoanalysis. Crashaw's intense ambivalence about pleasure and pain, purity and sin, permeates the rhetoric of his poetry, to the point where it becomes impossible to define his tone, attitude, and values[13] – all that Empson the pragmatist would like to know. Empson's theoretical statement on the difficulty of Crashaw's poetry is rich; it seems to sum up the problems I have been tracing. Speaking of Crashaw's opposed meanings, Empson writes:

are these *both* [i.e. the religious and the sexual] the context which is to define the opposites, or is he using one as a metaphor of the other, so that the ambiguity is of the first type, or each as a metaphor of each, so that it is of the third? Is he deceiving us about either, or just making a poem (detached from life) out of both? Is he generalising from two sorts of experience, or finding a narrow border of experience that both hold in common?   (217-18)

These rhetorical possibilities block pragmatic understanding. Is Crashaw serious about religion as sex? Is he merely being witty? Or, is he trying to solve a personal dilemma? The opposites could be reconciled in the individual poems according to any of the formulas Empson suggests, but we would remain uncertain about the correctness of the resolution. Read for their ambiguity, their multi-relevance, the poems could lead to a sense of detachment, not involvement, with our own desires. Read as a generalized comparison, an attitude widely applicable to life, the poetry may be deceiving us, luring us into either sin or morbid self-denial – two very unhappy prospects for the utilitarian Empson. Most difficult of all is telling whether or not we are thinking too seriously about mere wordplay (though a Derridean might deny even this distinction).

For once Empson verges uncomfortably close to a sense of alienation within the community of readers. He boldly claims that Crashaw illuminates "the most important thing about the communication of the arts," that is, our fundamental habit of thinking in terms of opposites. Oppositional thought should in principle maximize social satisfaction because it permits a wide range of possible responses. But the problem Empson seems to evade is agreement. Ambiguity becomes not flexibility of response but sheer multiplicity of response. In spite of our ability to disambiguate the words of Crashaw's poetry – to read it as a Type I – we nonetheless find that "any particular person reads it in any particular way" (220). Are we understanding Crashaw or ourselves? In a peculiar way, we cannot tell.

No reader can evade the dualism of Crashaw's poetry. *The Hymn to the Name and Honour of the admirable Sainte Teresa* joins sexual deflowering to divine love:

> Nor has she e'er yet understood
> Why to show love, she should shed blood,
> Yet though she cannot tell you why,
> She can love, and she can DY.

(Empson, 218)

We cannot tell if we are supposed to read this as a light sort of joke on Teresa's naivety, as a Type I ambiguity in which neither sex nor religion can claim the dominant meaning. Or is it rather some sort of generalization firmly linking together the morally perfect with the carnal? The equal prominence of the words "Love," "blood," and "DY" could be pointing to an unnamed, third level of reconciliation. Similarly, Crashaw's "translation" of the *Dies irae* gives us a "primitive" but very firm connection between Christian sympathy and the movement of the bowels:[14]

> O let thine own soft bowels pay
> Thy self; And so discharge that day.
> If sin can sigh, love can forgive.
> O say the word my Soul shall live.

(Empson, 222)

Empson really cannot tell whether this is generalized Type III, akin to the example from Shakespeare (and so a kind of witticism), or closer to the troubling sort of generalization found in Herbert, which defeats reconciliation as much as it invites it.

Crashaw's poetry must be seen as a form of generalization because it always involves two sorts of experience which it tries to broaden through mutual comparison. Neither side of our nature, the moral or the "grotesque" (as Empson calls it), may dominate the other. But perhaps this is pseudo-generalization because no common ground of meaning is discernible, except ambiguity itself and the fragmenting of the community of readers. The seventh type of ambiguity foreshadows not a greater utility for poetry but the psychoanalytically obsessed reader, a danger Empson would have wished to avoid. The attempt to subsume ambiguity under generalization cannot be carried out in good faith, though we may continue to admire Empson's benevolent ethical spirit. It is tempting to call his resort to generalization a critical blindness and to seek a deconstructive explanation. Such an explanation could be offered as soon as one begins to notice the highly aberrant, non-generalizable meaning of words such as "typical," "norm," and "common" in Empson's writing. But such an explanation would need to defend its own usefulness. It may turn out that the rhetorically wary, deconstructionist reader and the pragmatic reader are incompatible, in spite of so many current efforts to bring them together. The literary criticism of William Empson presents the strongest challenge I know to explain why.[15]

NOTES

1 I am referring to the discussion of Empson in W.K. Wimsatt and Cleanth Brooks, *Literary Criticism. A Short History* 2 vols. (1957; reprint Chicago: Univ. of Chicago Press 1978), 2: 64

2 Very recent criticism is beginning to notice the high degree to which Richards and Empson rely upon pragmatic criteria. See Colin MacCabe, "The Cambridge Heritage: Richards, Empson and Leavis," *Southern Review* 19 (1986): 243-9. Richards "insisted, from the beginning, on what one might term the *sociality* of language – the impossibility of analysing a purely linguistic element independently of whole series of features associated with its use. For Richards the analysis of language was always the analysis of discourse – of the specificity of the particular language use ... At a time when philosophers and linguists are paying more and more attention to the role of intention and the context of utterance in the analysis of language, it is well to remember that much contemporary discussion

merely recapitulates themes that Richards advanced sixty years ago."

3 Paul de Man, "The Dead-End of Formalist Criticism," in *Blindness and Insight*, 2nd ed. (Minneapolis: University of Minnesota Press 1983), 235.

4 For his specific discussion of these two theorists see "Some Versions of Rhetoric: Empson and de Man," in *The Contest of Faculties. Philosophy and Theory after Deconstruction* (London and New York: Methuen 1985), 70-96.

5 I choose the word "present" carefully, without any suggestion of the automatic possibility of resolving any ambiguity. Andrew Harrison, "Poetic Ambiguity," *Analysis* 23 (1963): 54-7, makes an interesting comparison between Empson's and Wittgenstein's treatment of logical contradictions. He regards *Seven Types* as he does the *Tractatus*: logical contradictions need not be assertions; they may be "presentations" of contradictions that reveal conditions of "truth-telling."

6 See Christopher Norris, *William Empson and the Philosophy of Literary Criticism* (London: The Athlone Press 1978), 79.

7 See A.E. Malloch, "The Unified Sensibility and Metaphysical Poetry," *College English* 15 (1953): 95-101. Malloch's essay is concerned with Empson only in passing, but its argument nevertheless bears greatly on the problems of Empson's approach to Metaphysical Poetry. Malloch draws a distinction between analogical techniques within various poems, which may be based on scholastic dialectics, simple punning, imagery, and so forth, and the much less easily definable "analogical" mode of sensibility, a mode that is "notoriously disrespectful to generic and specific boundaries." Thus the technical description of the way a particular metaphor functions may not necessarily lead to a generalizable conclusion about the nature of the poet's set of beliefs, even though the techniques draw the reader into a dialogical process. At the risk of pushing the analogy one disrespectful step further, one could argue as well that the same difficult gap is pointed to by de Man when he speaks of the problematic connection between the technicalities of poetics and the hermeneutical process of understanding the meaning of a text. See his essay on H.R. Jauss entitled "Reading and History'" in *The Resistance to Theory* (Minneapolis: University of Minnesota Press 1986), 54-72.

8 See Stanley Fish, "With the Compliments of the Author: Reflections on Austin and Derrida," *Critical Inquiry* 8 (1982): 693-721. Fish discusses the "pragmatic," "unformalizable" aspects of speech-act theory.

His essay in fact encompasses a much larger argument in favour of establishing a high degree of overlap between pragmatics and deconstruction. It attempts to mediate the ambiguities I allude to at the opening of this essay. Fish's argument includes references to John Searle, Walter Benn Michaels, Barbara Johnson, Mary Pratt, as well as Derrida and Aus-

tin; it is too wide-ranging to discuss in detail here and hinges on a notion
of "represented interpretation" which Fish claims is a common denomi-
nator in speech-act theory and in deconstruction. I would dispute this,
especially the suggestion that one can attach a strong definition of "representation" to deconstruction, but in the terminology I have been adapting
from Empson, one could say, briefly, that Fish favours "generalization"
over "ambiguity."

9 A good example of what I mean may be found in the last chapter of J. Hillis Miller's recent book *The Ethics of Reading. Kant, de Man, Eliot, Trollope,
James, and Benjamin* (New York: Columbia University Press 1987). The
chapter discusses James's preface to *The Golden Bowl*, specifically James's
pragmatic urge to do something socially useful with the act of writing, to
"do things with words" (Miller, 105). James treats the act of "putting
things into words" as an ethical one, a binding together of words that also
involves a binding together of social fabrics. But Miller, in exploring the
meaning of James's complex use of the terminology of "things," finds that
the effort to illuminate or glimpse the "thing" behind all social "things"
(be it self-renunciation or adultery) never becomes clear; the "thing" to be
glimpsed may be an act of betrayal, yet the mode of glimpsing that unspoken "thing" itself seems to be full of betrayal. Miller is not trying to
argue that James is an unethical writer. On the contrary. James's interest
in vague backgrounds and pragmatic understandings is never, in principle, fulfilled in his own writings, though the ethical imperative to name
the thing remains strong.

10 *Seven Types of Ambiguity*, revised ed. (New York: New Directions 1966), 1.
Further page references to this text will be made parenthetically within
the essay.

11 See, for example, R.S. Crane, "William Empson, Contemporary Criticism
and Poetic Diction," in *Critics and Criticism: Ancient and Modern*, ed. R.S.
Crane (1952; reprint Chicago: University of Chicago Press 1975), 29.

12 I have discussed Empson's dangerous tendency to generalize the tropes
of allegory and mutual metaphor, to make them into pseudo-normative
language functions, in two companion articles on the subject of typifica-
tion or "pregnancy" in *The Structure of Complex Words* (1953). See my "Empsonian Pregnancy in Wordsworth's Spousal Verse," *Dalhousie Review* 63
(1983): 555-65 and "Resistance and Pregnancy in Empsonian Metaphor,"
The British Journal of Aesthetics 26 (1986): 48-56.

13 I cite these terms in the technical senses attached to them by Richards
and Empson, which may be briefly summed up as the combination of the
speaker's attitudes to a statement, attitudes towards the listener, and the

speaker's purpose in speaking in a particular way. An outline of these divisions may be found in MacCabe, 242.

14 I put "translation" in quotation marks because this stanza has been inserted by Crashaw into his translation; of course it has no Latin counterpart. George Williams, Crashaw's most recent editor, can see no common meaning between sympathetic emotions and a "discharge," and by a neat paronomasia discharges the verse as "scatology" tastelessly mixed with "eschatology." See his *The Complete Poetry of Richard Crashaw*, (New York: New York University Press 1972), 191n.

15 An earlier, much more experimental version of this essay was read before the Cardiff Critical Theory Seminar, the University of Wales. An Andrew Mellon Postdoctoral Fellowship and a travel grant, both awarded by the Department of English, the Johns Hopkins University, supported the preparation of the early version of this essay.

DEAN FRYE

Custom and Utterance in *Hamlet*

We must speak by the card, or equivocation will undo us.

As a play in which the hero's central act occurs towards the very end, *Hamlet* concerns itself to an unusual degree with the sources of action. In *Macbeth*, in contrast, with its early regicide, the emphasis is upon consequences, and upon the fact that what is done cannot be undone. But while "done" echos through *Macbeth* like a tolling bell, most of *Hamlet* takes place while "this thing's to do," and generates a fair amount of uncertainty that it will ever be done at all. The many explanations that have been offered for this doubtful situation – logistical, conventional, moral, characterizational, psychoanalytical – are in no way mutually exclusive and are not diminished by laying stress on Hamlet's own preoccupation, among so many, with establishing the proper relationship between action and the acting self: with the possibility of act as authentic utterance. Of Shakespeare's other tragic heroes, only Brutus concerns himself with such puzzling, and potentially paralyzing, speculations, which finally involve the meaning, or the possibility, of human freedom. It is in Hamlet's nature, and consequently in *Hamlet*'s nature (the placing of the italics is arbitrary) to be so concerned, however, and this concern is related to, and given a context by, ideas about custom.

This preoccupation is evident almost as soon as Hamlet speaks. If death of fathers is common, asks Gertrude, "Why seems it so particular with thee?" (I. ii. 75).[1] She means something like "why is it, as it seems to me, so particular," but Hamlet seizes upon the "seems" as if he had just discovered the Theme of Appearance vs. Reality. Sharply contrasting "seems" and "is," he naturally insists that outward signs of grief – sighs, tears, and inky cloak – cannot denote him truly, being "actions that a man might play" (76–84). But since there would seem to be no language, gesture, dress, or utterance of any kind that a man might *not* play, the possibility of denoting oneself truly is at best severely limited, if Hamlet is right that the theatrical is the opposite of the true. Actions that can be played and understood may seem lifelessly conventional, a medium of exchange debased by hypocritical players, but after all communication, if not expression itself, depends upon convention. The "forms, moods, shapes of grief" may involve a fashioning consciousness which intrudes between passionate self and its expression, but can true expression be limited to the most instinctive, undifferentiated and depersonalized utterances, like howls? Still, the conventions of expression are limiting. Hamlet's first soliloquy (I. ii. 129–159) makes clear the true source of his grief, but since there is no conventional dress to express shock at the hasty and incestuous remarriage of one's mother, he has had to fall back upon customary suits of solemn black as the closest approximation the language of clothing provides. With his anxieties about the authenticity of his own utterance, it is no wonder that despite his famous loquacity Hamlet feels himself to be tongue-tied for much of the play.

They handle these things better in the Polonius family, having their way to make in the world. Polonius's advice to Laertes (I. iii. 59–80) is persuasive as a set of precepts for a man on the rise in a slippery and chaotic world. Laertes, upward bound to nowhere in particular as yet, is to prepare himself by establishing a character of prudence and solidity as, apparently, if surprisingly, his father has done. A garrulous and silly version of the middle-class privy councillor, an unsagacious Cecil or inefficiently devious Walsingham, Polonius is at least as much an Elizabethan "new man" as Edmund in *King Lear*, though of a different sort. If Edmund, as he announces himself to the audience at the beginning of I. ii, objectifies the fears and fascination of aggressive individualism, as John F. Danby suggested,[2] Polonius presents a less flamboyant but more familiar image of self-interested adaptation. Both believe in the manipulation of appearance and the premeditated control of expression for effect; both understand the importance of creating a role. The difference lies in the nature of the self behind the mask. The stage Machiavel is always intensely aware of a true self, exactly the opposite of what he seems, and expresses it occasionally in soliloquy. For Polonius, the relation between self and expression, and indeed the very nature of the self to which one should be true, is less clearly defined. A Polonian soliloquy is as hard to imagine as *Hamlet* without the Prince of Denmark *solus*.

Certainly, in the Polonian system, there are thoughts that should be given no tongue and judgment to be reserved. Certainly, one assumes one's "habit" as a kind of theatrical costume: "Costly ... But not expressed in fancy, rich, not gaudy" (70–1). Translations of this precept into contemporary parlance are widely available: "By understanding impression management through appearance you can begin to plan your appearance and package yourself to generate an automatic positive response from those you meet in business and social situations."[3] If Laertes shows a youthful fancifulness in his costume that Polonius is mildly reproving, the humour in the idea that the recommended apparel will "proclaim" him is that much more evident. But such dress is less a matter of disguise than of choosing the clothing one wishes to grow into, and the whole Polonian program suggests less the dissimulation than the creation of the self, which complicates the process of expression. The idea of authentic utterance assumes the existence of a defined self which may be represented, or misrepresented, in behaviour. Hamlet's search for a language which can denote him truly begins in the desire for integrity and becomes a strategy for self-discovery. But for Polonius, expression is to some extent prior to the self to be formed by it. He advocates a low-level form of what Stephen Greenblatt calls "self-fashioning,"[4] but one that aims at a very conventional self through a process of habituation. "Self-conditioning" more nearly describes it.

This force of habit is an acknowledged fact, whatever attitude is taken to it, and a pervasive Elizabethan theme. The word "custom" covered both our usual senses of it and much that we would call "habit" – though mourning dress is conventional, Hamlet's suits of solemn black are "customary" in the sense of being habitually worn – and there are constant references to "the tyrant custom," "that vice-nature custome," "that Universal Tyrant of the earth," and the like.[5] "Custom," says Bacon, "is the principal magistrate of man's life," and is most powerful when "it beginneth in young years: this we call education, which is, in effect, but an early custom."[6] Man's deeds are the result of habit, and "therefore as Machiavel well noteth (though in an evil-favoured instance), there is no trusting to the force of nature nor to the bravery of words, except it be corroborate by custom."[7] Machiavelli is not, of course, original here. While "intellectual virtue owes both its birth and its growth to teaching," Aristotle had written, "moral virtue comes about as a result of habit, whence also its name *ethike* is one that is formed by a slight variation from the word *ethos*" (Eth. Nic. 2.1. 1103a14–18).[8] The power of moral argument is limited – "argument and teaching, we may suspect, are not powerful with all men" (10.9. 1179b23–4) – and nature provides a necessary but not sufficient cause of virtue: "Neither by nature ... nor contrary to nature do the virtues arise in us; rather we are adapted by nature to receive them, and are made perfect by habit" (2.1. 1103a23–5). "Therefore," says Bacon, "let men by all means endeavor to obtain good customs."[9]

One way of obtaining good customs is enacting good laws, which may begin in coercion but can then produce good habits, though in fact much law recognized or codified extant custom. When a positive law aims at overturning an established custom, however, the conflict may be variously judged.[10] Bacon tends to be conservative here. "It is true," he writes in "Of Innovations," "that what is settled by custom, though it be not good, yet at least it is fit," and it is therefore best "not to try experiments in states, except the necessity be urgent, or the utility evident."[11] Even Montaigne, who regularly opposes custom to reason and finds that "no fantasie so mad can fall into humane imagination, that meets not with the example of some publick custome,"[12] still doubts "whether any so evident profit may be found in the change of a received law, of what nature soever, as there is hurt in removing the same."[13] Safety lies in established practice, as John Hall wrote:

> For custome (Aristotle sayth)
> Is lyke to an other nature
> So that he whiche him therin staith,
> Hath good assurance long to dure.[14]

It may be true, as Leonard Nathanson says, that "the concepts of *nomos* (custom or convention) and *physis* (nature) ... implied not only the distinction between physical phenomena and human invention, but also the opposition between what is objective and according to universal natural law and what is subjective and according to particular and erroneous opinion,"[15] but the denigration of custom is often a sign of villainy, and in fact the rejection of morality and religion as mere opinion reinforced by custom is a standard part of the technique of Circe's many descendants in the Renaissance. As R.C. Bald has shown,[16] Edmund has much villainous precedent in appealing to nature against "the plague of custom" (*Lear* I. ii. 3). The conservative sense of the danger of such an appeal may be based on a simple assumption of the naturalness of one's own customs, but in men like Bacon and Montaigne it reflects a scepticism about the general efficacy of human reason.

Explicable as such conservative scepticism may be, however, it obviously runs contrary to widely expressed beliefs about the potential

dignity of man, a dignity based upon his reason and his freedom. Edmund's appeal to a Hobbesian state of nature, as if it were the Golden
Age, may appal the virtuous, but what of the appeal to nature as the
object of right reason, as truth? As Milton was to say, custom "rests not
in her unaccomplishment until by secret inclination she accorporate
herself with error," so that "error supports custom, custom counte-
nances error; and these two between them would persecute and chase
away all truth and solid wisdom out of human life," if it were not for
periodic reforms.[17] And if Milton's attitude towards the tyrant custom is
predictable, consider Coriolanus on the requirement that he appear
before the people in the "napless vesture of humility" (*Corio* II. i. 234):

> Custom calls me to't.
> What custom wills, in all things should we do't,
> The dust on antique time would lie unswept,
> And Mountainous error be too highly heap'd
> For truth to o'erpeer.   (II. iii. 117–21)

The claims of the rational over the habitual may have had more plausible champions, but Coriolanus is giving radical expression to an unex-
ceptionable view of the limits of custom. The vast spring cleaning of the
human mind and vocabulary which is the Baconian program is based
upon the same perception.

The wealth of Renaissance material on odd customs of other peoples,
so interesting to people like Montaigne and Browne, severely weak-
ened, or at least limited, the idea of the *consensus gentium*, the collective
wisdom embodied in universal custom.[18] Where there was so little consensus, custom lost much of its authority, except as a matter of convenience in indifferent matters. In morals, the dangers of custom were
stressed as often as the utility of virtuous habits. Hooker finds in vi-
cious habituation a main impediment to virtue, since "custom inuring
the mind by long practice, and so leaving there a sensible impression,
prevaileth more than reasonable persuasion what way soever,"[19] so that
the will is led against the dictates of the reason, custom here replacing
the more usual passion as the usurper. As the Old Man says to Marlowe's Faustus, "Yet, yet, thou hast an amiable soul / If sin by custom
grow not into nature."[20] The danger, and the attraction, of custom
grown second nature is that it excuses one from listening to reason. In
Thomas Lovell's *Dialogve between Custom and Veritie*, Truth may score all
the debating points, but Custom has its own resources:

Though all my proof thou hast disproov'd
  and I no proof can bring:
This shift I haue, say what thou wilt
  I wil beleeue nothing.[21]

Many literary instances of evil "customs" reflect a certain perverse wilfulness associated with the word, especially when the practices are not properly customs at all. The sacrificing of virgins to appease Neptune, in Lyly's *Gallathea*, is called "the custom of this country,"[22] but it is "the custom, the bloody custom, ordained for the safety of the country" (v. ii. 11–12). *The Custom of the Country*, in the Beaumont and Fletcher canon, deals with a sort of *droit de seigneur* – "the wicked Custom of this Country / The barbarous, most inhuman, damned custom"[23] – which, however, the Governor could after all waive if he wished. The point is clear when Spenser's Calidore encounters the castle of Briana, "Which doth obserue a custome lewd and ill,"[24] involving shaving the beards or hair of passing knights and ladies. "A shamefull vse as euer I did heare, / Sayde Calidore" (i. 14), but the practice is neither an old folkway nor a bad habit; it is quite purposeful. Briana is one of those who "breake bands of ciuilitie, / And wicked customes make," (i. 26), and, having made them, follow them as if relieved of the responsibility of choice. The master of this process is Tamburlaine, with his elaborate ritual of siege which leads, if a city delays yielding, to universal slaughter on the third day. This "custom proper to his sword, / Which he observes as parcel of his fame – Intending so to terrify the world"[25] is his recent invention, but Tamburlaine considers himself bound by it. He is sorry for the victims, and angry at their leaders for not yielding earlier: "They know my custom" (67). This is really a matter of a vow deemed unbreakable, but the insistent use of "custom" relates two ways of wilfully avoiding the responsibility of choice: "And know my customs are as peremptory / As wrathful planets, death, or destiny" (127).

In this element of mechanization, of a disengagement of self from action, which in different contexts is one definition of the comic, lies an ethical problem which cannot be solved by the substitution of good customs for bad, any more than virtue can be externally coerced. And while it is reason that is normally said to be the superior source of action, "reason" refers less to the intellect than to the underlying, integrated, authentic self, beneath habit and momentary emotion, but including conviction and commitment. Or so it seems to Hamlet. Certainly, when Meric Casaubon came to sum up the whole subject of custom, and to insist upon the ultimate distinction between custom and truth, it was to champion the cause of reason. While accepting both the power and the utility of the customary, with all the usual examples and a wealth of classical and patristic citations, and while admitting paradoxically that, since it is "the nature of sublunarie things, to be altered by *custome* ... when *custome* hath once through continuance naturalized her selfe into any of them, then *custome* (to speake properly:) is no more custome, but Nature,"[26] Casaubon nevertheless insists that to speak of "a man that is led by custome and not by reason" is really to speak of "a thing that hath the shape of a man, but may more truly & properly be called a brute" (186–7). And certainly Hamlet, wishing to act authentically and not merely conventionally, and finding himself unable to act at all, accuses himself of some failure of reason:

> What is a man,
> If his chief good and market of his time
> Be but to sleep and feed? a beast, no more.
> Sure He that made us with such large discourse,
> Looking before and after, gave us not
> That capability and godlike reason
> To fust in us unus'd.   (IV. iv. 33–9)

But just as it was not in any simple sense his reason that could not be denoted by actions that a man might play, so the act of revenge he seeks would express the totality of the self to which he would be true, in the profound sense of the Polonian commonplace.

Hamlet's views of custom reflect this commitment to the ideal of free act, as in the case of Claudius's flamboyant bibulosity, with its accompaniment of drums, trumpets, and cannons. "Is it a custom?" asks Horatio, suggesting that if so that would excuse a lot (I. iv. 12), but for Hamlet "it is a custom more honor'd in the breach than the observance" (15–16). This leads to the "dram of eale" speech, in which "some habit, that too much o'er-leavens / The form of plausive manners" (29–30) is naturally among the defects that can corrupt the reputation. Similarly, the Gravedigger singing at his work lacks, for Hamlet, a proper solemnity. "Custom," says Horatio, "hath made it in him a property of easiness" (V. i. 67–8), which for the young men is a deadening of natural response, though Hamlet has the grace to recognize that finer feelings are in part a leisure-class prerogative (69–70). And in his confrontation with his mother, he will wring her heart "If damned custom have not brass'd it so / That it be proof and bulwark against sense" (III. iv. 37–8).

In Gertrude's case, however, lacking faith in her firmness of mind, Hamlet will countenance the support, and even in a sense the creation, of virtue by custom:

> go not to my uncle's bed –
> Assume a virtue, if you have it not.
> That monster custom, who all sense doth eat,
> Of habits devil, is angel yet in this,
> That to the use of actions fair and good
> He likewise gives a frock or livery
> That aptly is put on. Refrain to-night,
> And that shall lend a kind of easiness
> To the next abstinence, the next more easy;
> For use almost can change the stamp of nature.   (159–68)

The use of clothing imagery here is of course practically inevitable; dress and custom are constantly associated. "Costume," after all, shares its etymology with "custom," just as "habit" is the same word in its various senses. It is defined in one early dictionary both as "a qualitie in the bodie or minde, not naturall, but gotten by long custome" and as the "outward attire of the bodie, whereby one person may be distinguished from another; as the habit of a Gentleman, is different from the habit of a merchant, and the habit of a Handi-crafts man differing from them both."[27] Convention strictly limits the range of individual choice in dress, whether or not the wearer realizes it, if it does not eliminate choice entirely by imposing a uniform, and Elizabethan sumptuary laws aimed at codifying a simple relation between rank and clothing in an almost theatrically costumed society. If clothes can to some extent proclaim a personal self, the expression must still be decipherable within the conventions of the dress code, and will readily become habitual. Clothing is also an important symbol of the artificial, as is all the dressing – of gardens, of food, of hair – that modifies fallen nature for human purposes, just as custom is ultimately artificial, however comfortable the garment may become through wear. What Hamlet recommends to Gertrude, in an uncharacteristic moment of Polonianism, is abstinence, not as the natural expression, but as the artificial fashioner, of a virtuous self. But custom is primarily a devil to him, even if he must compact with it in fitting himself for the revenger's role.

In the nature of this role is a problematical relationship between self and act. Revenge is not simply a debt to be paid. Like a religious vocation, it requires the concentration of the faculties upon action which is not, in any usual sense, self-interested, and this is a conversion which involves profound changes in identity, at least in the sense of radical simplification and focusing:

> Yea, from the table of my memory
> I'll wipe away all trivial fond records,
> All saws of books, all forms, all pressures past
> That youth and observation copied there,
> And thy commandment all alone shall live
> Within the book and volume of my brain,
> Unmix'd with baser matter.   (I. v. 98–104)

If the new self implied by such radical editing of the memory bank is to have the authenticity of endurance, it must be based upon more than momentary passion or mechanical custom. "Purpose," as the Player King says, "is but the slave to memory" (III. ii. 188), so that "What to ourselves in passion we propose, /The passion ending, doth the purpose lose" (194–5). Claudius makes a similar point while fashioning Laertes into an avenger: "That we would do, / We should do when we would; for this 'would' changes, / And hath abatements and delays as many / As there are tongues, are hands, are accidents" (IV. vii. 118–21). And if passionate vows will not serve, neither, for one to whom role and self are as antithetical as "seems" and "is," will adherence to customary speech, gesture, or action that a man might play.

But Hamlet seems to think that he owes it to himself to try, when his original commitment loses its edge. Unable now to feel revenge as authentic utterance, yet unwilling or unable to change his outer resolve, he sporadically attempts to alter himself through experiments with the conventional role of the stage revenger, as defined by Kyd's Hieronimo and, perhaps, more relevantly by his own previous manifestation in the Ur-Hamlet. Whether or not real avengers find themselves adopting ritualized, theatrical gestures, the typical stage revenger customarily plays a predictable part of conventionalized unconventionality. The preoccupation with theatre in Hamlet, with its stage metaphors and professional chat, is well known, and William Empson long ago pointed out that a central effect of this is to emphasize the distance between the heroes of this updated Hamlet and an older, more straightforwardly theatrical version, and thus to create an elaborate theatrical metaphor that exactly reinforces Hamlet's story.[28] Realistically speaking, Hamlet is by intelligence and education an improbable avenger; dramatically, he is a character even more ludicrously unsuited to the role as customarily played.

His attempts to think himself into the role and to feel the part – to generate the emotion for which the act of revenge will be a sort of objective correlative – only emphasize the cursed spite in his casting and his own almost certain artistic failure.

Primarily, these attempts involve experiments with language, the trying on of customary garments of style. Hamlet has a range of authentic styles, of which that of the "To be or not to be" soliloquy seems most truly to denote him, with its quiet depth of puzzlement and its structure of intellectual disputation. But he is also a good mimic, and can win the contest in Marlovian hyperbole at Ophelia's graveside hands down. Laertes, that conventional young man, has adapted to his new role as readily as he adopts the style of an earlier, more innocently rhetorical dramatic period:

> Now pile your dust upon the quick and dead,
> Till of this flat a mountain you have made
> T'o'ertop old Pelion, or the skyish head
> Of blue Olympus.   (v. i. 251–4)

This is a game Hamlet can play, as he notes with considerable complacency:

> And if thou prate of mountains let them throw
> Millions of acres on us, till our ground,
> Singeing his pate against the burning zone,
> Make Ossa like a wart! Nay, and thou'lt mouth,
> I'll rant as well as thou.   (280–4)

Whatever Hamlet's feelings at this moment, we know that they cannot be truly expressed like this. More momentarily genuine are his words after the play scene:

> 'Tis now the very witching time of night,
> When churchyards yawn and hell itself breathes out
> Contagion to this world. Now could I drink hot blood,
> And do such bitter business as the day
> Would quake to look on.   (iii. ii. 388–92)

But as with the nocturnal atmospherics of Macbeth which the lines anticipate, these images are partly Hamlet's attempt to get himself into the mood, just as Macbeth would not hear his footsteps approaching

Duncan's chamber, lest they "take the present horror from the time, / Which now suits with it" (II. i. 59–60).

In his soliloquy after the First Player's recitation (II. ii. 549–605), in the midst of the densest concentration of theatrical references in the play, Hamlet again addresses the relation between playing and being and momentarily reverses, not very logically, his usual conception of the priority of self over utterance. The Player, experiencing emotion generated out of mere words, forcing his soul to his own conceit, suggests an aspect of the actor's art that is beyond technical craft and reminds us that playing may be a metaphor for relations between self and expression more complicated than simple hypocrisy. But in imagining him, "Had he the motive and the cue for passion / That I have" (561–2), Hamlet loses the complicated sense of the metaphor, turning the Player into just a man capable of passion. "He would drown the stage with tears, / And cleave the general ear with horrid speech, / Make mad the guilty, and apall the free" (562–4). He would, in fact, out-herod Herod, expressing his feelings in precisely the acting style which Hamlet will shortly advise the actors to avoid (III. ii. 1–45), perhaps with a glance at the Lord Admiral's company's staging of Marlowe and *The Spanish Tragedy*. Such a style, failing in its proper end "to hold as 'twere the mirror up to nature" (21–2), can communicate only the most simplified feeling, certainly by 1601; as a pattern on which to fashion self, it would create internally the sort of monstrosity that has led Hamlet, watching bad actors, to think "some of Nature's journeymen had made men ... they imitated humanity so abominably" (33–5). But he will try anything, so convinced is he that there is some basic lack in him

> or ere this
> I should 'a' fatted all the region kites
> With this slave's offal. Bloody, bawdy villain!
> Remorseless, treacherous, lecherous, kindless villain!
> (II. ii. 578–81)

The prosiness of "all the region kites," and the infelicity of "bloody, bawdy" and, especially, "treacherous, lecherous," reminiscent of Bottom's *Pyramus and Thisbe*, make this exactly the kind of theatre Hamlet denigrates. The First Folio's following half-line – "Oh Vengeance!" – seems right in producing an appropriate crescendo before Hamlet gives up the attempt and the speech suddenly quiets: "Why, what an ass am I!" (582). Externally "prompted" to the act of revenge, he has instead unpacked his heart with words like a whore, the simulator of passion who now becomes the type of the player. Hamlet turns to plotting, but his problem is still unsolved.

It is, in fact, never so much solved as dissolved. After his return from the sea, Hamlet appears to have come to terms with his situation by placing himself in the hands of the providence that ordains the fall of a sparrow (v. ii. 220), the "divinity that shapes our ends" (10). But in as specifically Christian a play as this, the relation of divinity to revenge raises as many questions as it answers, just as there was something too easy in Hamlet's avoidance of responsibility for Polonius's death: "heaven hath pleas'd it so / To punish me with this, and this with me, / That I must be their scourge and minister" (III. iv. 173-5). His newfound submission cures his desire for a humanly impossible control of eventualities, but the very un-Miltonic God to which he turns, willing to shoulder all the responsibility and take back the terrible gift of freedom, represents a turning away from his most basic convictions in order to play out his role. Providence, in a play - or Time, or Nature, or whatever force is deemed to shape the ends of the characters - is after all provided by the playwright, or rather, especially in Shakespeare's case, by the underlying structure of the narrative or dramatic form which the playwright discovers and realizes. One of the common meanings of "the world's a stage," as in Jaques's speech (*As You Like It* II. vii. 139-66), is deterministic: our parts are written for us, and by a not particularly experimental Dramatist. Hamlet becomes like those comic heroines who wisely swim with the current towards the inevitable, and somehow natural, happy ending. The force that drives the revenge play, however, a curiously specialized form of popular drama, feels more artificial than natural and has the inevitability only of its own obtrusive conventions. Hamlet finally lacks the heroic simplicity to destroy the form, though he comes close to doing so at times, stretching it almost to the breaking point, resisting much of its customary style and gesture with the impossible demand that the act of revenge be the authentic utterance of an integrated self. He thus figures forth in a most extreme manner the pain and perplexity of such a quest, before the customary and conventional claim him and absorb him into the pattern:

Here, thou incestious, murd'rous, damned Dane,
Drink off this potion! Is thy union here?
Follow my mother!   [King dies]   (v. ii. 325-7)

NOTES

1 Shakespearean references are to *The Riverside Shakespeare*, ed. G. Blakemore Evans (Boston: Houghton Mifflin 1974).

2 John F. Danby, *Shakespeare's Doctrine of Nature* (London: Faber and Faber 1961), 43–53.

3 William Thourlby, *You Are What You Wear* (New York: New American Library 1978), 34.

4 Stephen Greenblatt, *Renaissance Self-Fashioning From More to Shakespeare* (Chicago: University of Chicago Press 1980).

5 *Othello*, I. iii. 229; John Donne, "Loves Deitie" in *Poems*, ed. Sir Herbert Grierson (London: Oxford University Press 1933), 48; Samuel Daniel, *The Queenes Arcadia* 2563 in *Complete Works*, ed. Alexander B. Grosart, 5 vols. (1885–96), 3:299.

6 Francis Bacon, "Of Custom and Education," in *Francis Bacon: A Selection of his Works*, ed. Sidney Warhaft (Toronto: Macmillan 1965), 149.

7 Ibid., 148.

8 Aristotle, trans. W.D. Ross, in *Basic Works*, ed. Richard McKeon (New York: Random House 1941).

9 Bacon, "Of Innovations," in *Francis Bacon: A Selection of his Works*, ed. Sidney Warhaft (Toronto: Macmillan 1965), 108–9.

10 Michael D. Bristol cites *A Breefe Discourse, declaring and appouing the necessarie and inviolable maintenance of certain laudable custemes of London* (1584) in *Carnival and Theater* (London: Methuen 1985), 86.

11 Bacon, "Of Custom and Education," 108, 109.

12 Michel de Montaigne, "Of Custome, And How a Received Law Should Not Easily Be Changed," in *Essayes*, trans. John Florio (New York: Modern Library 1933), 76.

13 Ibid., 84.

14 *The Court of Virtue* (1565), ed. Russell A. Fraser (New Brunswick, NJ: Rutgers University Press 1961), 247.

15 Leonard Nathanson, *The Strategy of Truth: A Study of Sir Thomas Browne* (Chicago: University of Chicago Press 1967), 60.

16 R.C. Bald, " 'Thou, Nature, Art My Goddess': Edmund and Renaissance Free-Thought," *Joseph Quincy Adams Memorial Studies*, eds. James G. McManaway, Giles E. Dawson, Edwin E. Willoughby (Washington: The Folger Library 1948), 337–49.

17 John Milton, *The Doctrine and Discipline of Divorce*, in *Prose Selections*, ed. Merritt Y. Hughes (New York: Odyssey Press 1947), 161–2.

18 On this see Margaret T. Hodgen, *Early Anthropology in the Sixteenth and Seventeenth Centuries* (Philadelphia: University of Pennsylvania Press 1964).

19 Richard Hooker, *Of The Laws of Ecclesiastical Polity*, 2 vols. (London: Every-man's Library 1907), 1:172, 173.

20 Christopher Marlowe, *Doctor Faustus*, v. i. 37-8, in *Plays*, ed. Leo Kirsch-baum (Cleveland, OH: World Publishing 1962).

21 Thomas Lovell, *Dialogue between Custom and Veritie* (London, 1581), 20.

22 John Lyly, *Gallathea*, I. i. 66; in *Gallathea and Midas*, ed. Anne Begor Lanca-shire (Lincoln: University of Nebraska Press 1969).

23 Francis Beaumont and John Fletcher, *The Custom of the Country*, I. i. 20-1, in *Works*, ed. George Darby (London: George Routledge 1876), 1:106.

24 Edmund Spenser, *The Faerie Queene* VI. i. 13, in *Poetical Works*, ed. J.C. Smith and E. de Selincourt (Oxford: Oxford University Press 1912).

25 Christopher Marlowe, *1 Tamburlaine* v. i. 13-15 (see note 20).

26 Meric Casaubon, *A Treatise of Vse and Cvstome* (London, 1638), 61.

27 John Bullokar, *An English Expositor* (1616) (Menston, England: Scolar Press 1967), under "habit."

28 William Empson, "*Hamlet* When New Part I," *Sewanee Review* 61, no. 1 (1953): 19-31.

Portraits, Effigies, and the
Narrative Impulse

Stay, mortal, Stay: and look upon
The language of a speaking stone
– from the epitaph of Dr. James Vaulx

When *An Apologie for Poetry* was first published in 1595, Sidney had been dead nine years. The late publication of the *Apologie* allows us to think Sidney's voice much fresher in the earlier seventeenth century than might otherwise have been the case; yet by then an important part of the aesthetic structure to which Sidney referred was within a few years of being swept away. Had Dr Vaulx raised a monument to *his* father in (let us suppose) the year the *Apologie* was printed, it would have differed substantially from the early Caroline monument his son in fact raised to him. The nature and extent of that difference mark an entire revolution in taste, rendered in small. A significant part of that revolution was the supplanting of the high Elizabethan portrait style by the three-dimensional realism which long had marked continental painting. An unlooked-for consequence was a substantial reduction in the ability of portraits, as visual texts, to direct their own interpetation, despite the appearance of greater accessibility in their lively faces and increasingly easy poses. Sidney, whose portrait was painted by Paolo Veronese in February of 1574,[1] had some acquaintance with these effects even though they were largely invisible to his English contemporaries. Although later he questioned Hilliard on the techniques involved, Sidney probably did not know fully how the effect of dimensionality was managed,[2] but his speculations on the artist and his subject leave little doubt that he sensed some of the consequences.

In the *Apologie* Sidney makes few claims for poetry so notable as the assertion that poets figure forth a landscape which far excels in perfection the landscape we ordinarily see.

Onely the Poet ... lifted vp with the vigor of his owne inuention, dooth growe in effect another nature, in making things either better then Nature bringeth forth, or, quite a newe, forms such as neuer were in Nature ... : so as hee goeth hand in hand with Nature, not inclosed within the narrow warrant of her guifts, but freely ranging onely within the Zodiak of his owne wit. Nature neuver set forth the earth in so rich tapistry as diuers poets haue done ...[3]

The ease with which Sidney reaches for the visual analogy to the poets' art speaks to the close connection between the two and invites us to test one form by what we think we know about the other. It may suggest that both the making and the perception of visual objects are in some important respects the same acts, regardless of the physical form those objects take – whether they are on the stage, or contained within a verbal image, or carved and painted as a portrait bust. If so, it implies that maker and reader have an analogous relationship to the texts they confront. Sidney's remark introduces a discussion of the connection between text and narrative rescription which is more familiar in litera-ture than in the visual arts and which is far from being resolved.

Sidney's poet goes "hand in hand with nature," but his narrative of the object of his attention is "not enclosed within the narrow warrant of her guifts." Those two phrases set the dimensions of a practical and ethical dilemma for the reader-poet, who would not be like "the meaner sort of Painters (who counterfet onely such faces as are sette before them)," but like "the more excellent, who, hauing no law but wit, be-stow that in cullours vpon you which is fittest for the eye to see" (159). As a perspective on going hand in hand with nature, this raises more questions than it answers. Where is the text, if it is not in those surfaces which the meaner sort of painters counterfeit, and how is it to be rendered if not by counterfeiting? What shapes and controls the artist's access to it? What capacity has the text to control its own interpretation at the hands of an artist freed to bestow upon you what is "fittist for the eye to see?" What ability has the ensuing work to control its interpreta-tion at the hands of those who confront it? Or to put the matter another way, what constrains response? how far can you go? These are ques-tions of some general application.

Early in the reign of Charles I, Francis Vaulx – the eldest son of Dr James Vaulx – caused a monument to be erected at St Mary's Church in the Cotswold village of Meysey Hampton (fig. 1). The year was 1630, some three years after the death of his father, whose effigy occupies the monument's centre panel, and perhaps a decade or a little more after Shakespeare's monument had been put up at Stratford (fig. 2). The two effigies show what seems to be a striking difference in liveliness.

Shakespeare's is frozen, immobile. Vaulx's is full of expression. How did they come to be so different, and do their differences have wider implications? Do they, for example, tell us something about differences between Elizabethan and Caroline reponses to visual cues, or about differences in the cues themselves?

To Samuel Shoenbaum, this lack of liveliness is an obtrusive feature of the Shakespeare effigy. He attributes it to the rigidities of Jacobean style.[4] In a recent article on the *Flower Portrait*, Paul Bertram and Frank Cossa make a different and slightly deflating speculation: that the carver took Shakespeare's features from a death mask.[5] There is no direct evidence for this, but the idea is persuasive. Certainly, the preternatural stillness of Shakespeare's face in the effigy could be accounted for that way. But no matter how that stillness came to be, it interferes far more with our sense of the portrait's "realism" than it seems to have done at the time. At least, to make an old argument, the portrait had to be accepted by Shakespeare's family as a reasonable representation of the man. Despite the pronounced unliveliness of the face, in which it is so different from the representation of Dr Vaulx, and the lack of correspondence with other portraits of Shakespeare, it seems clear they accepted the representation. Why was that?

The decade that lies between the portrait bust of Shakespeare and that of Dr Vaulx is important, not because it places Shakespeare's effigy on one side of a stylistic divide and Vaulx's on another, but because a comparison of the two shows them to be at two stages in a rapid development of style toward the modern notion that likeness is nearly wholly dependent on the rendering of the face. Van Dyck made this style so popular in England after he established his London studio in 1626 that "face painting" came to supplant the Elizabethan "limning" in the vocabulary of the period. This marks the movement from portraits as imitations of their sitters' condition to the imitation of their faces.

In tomb architecture, this change in what is imitated carries forward from the medieval figure of the recumbent knight (and frequently his dessicated corpse), depicting less the man than the lesson of mortality, to the individualized and lively portrait bust of Dr Vaulx and beyond. The effigy of Sir Thomas Hoby (All Saints', Bisham, Berks., ca 1570) is still in this general style, without the emblems of mortality. By the turn of the century or a little earlier, however, recumbent figures often rise on one elbow (John Dixon, St Phillip's, Little Rollright, Oxon.), a pose to which Webster's Bosola adverts as looking as if they had died of the toothache.[6] They sometimes are shown kneeling before prayer desks

(John Dormer and his wife, St James, Rousham, Oxon.), their own tombs (Garrard Monument, St James, Dorney, Bucks., ca 1610) or their gravestones (Stephen[s?] Wisdom, St Kenelm's, Church Enstone, Oxon., 1633). Poses become relaxed and sometimes strikingly informal: a couple sit in relaxed and chatty conversation (subsidiary figures on the tomb of Sir Henry and Lady Anne Poole, St Kenelm, Sapperton, Glos., 1616) or hold hands across a double *prie-dieu* (George Monox and his wife, St John the Baptist, Cirencester, Glos., 1638). Faces become individualized and given the skill of the carver, very lifelike (Vaulx, 1630 or Edward Dixon and his wives, St Phillip's, Little Rollright, 1647). The transition is characterized by the giving way of the generalized moral statement to the representation of the individual, but the statement of condition continues, although progressively more overshadowed by the attention given to the face. There is, of course, much overlapping of styles in each stage; but the movement is clear, and it brings tomb effigies like that of Dr Vaulx into some harmony with portrait style in the same period.

Vaulx's portrait exhibits both the lively, realistic face which Van Dyck popularized and some emblematic elements of the sort which were characteristic of the high Elizabethan style and which Van Dyck also included in his portraits. In the Vaulx effigy, these appear as conventional elements in a *memento mori* portrait or possibly as the normal accoutrements of a physician's study. This disguises, if only thinly, a conventional element of tomb effigies – the skull which indicates that the subject was dead when the effigy was erected – and thus draws the effigy nearer to a portrait of a living man, inverting the joke contained in the doctor's name and explained in his epitaph: "... & Thou mayest greeving knowe, / That none but Vaulx can lie below."

When we see Vaulx between his two wives, the effect is so startling that it irresistibly summons a narrative. Vaulx's first wife, Edith Jinner, is to the left as we view the monument. His second, Philip(pa?) Horton, is to the right (fig. 1). It would be hard to imagine a greater contrast than the effigies of these two women seem to represent. The one is something of a beauty, almost ethereal. The other belongs plainly enough to another order altogether. How did they both come to occupy parts of the life of the man whose effigy rests between theirs? These are contrasts or perhaps discontinuities which it is our overwhelming instinct to bridge, to provide some story which will account for the disjuncture. When we do so, we launch ourselves upon a very uncertain imaginative enterprise.

The issue here is not whether Vaulx is really asking himself the ques-

tion we think we know he is, or even how the portraits of these two
ladies came to differ so much from each other, and in one case, very
possibly so much from herself. To that end, it would be necessary to
supply another narrative, not only about Vaulx's life, but both about his
son's perception of it and the manner in which the tomb was made. It is
almost irresistible to do so, to think of the emotions with which the son
confronted his stepmother, of romantic memories of his own mother
which led him to supply the carver with a painting of Edith Jinner as a
young matron, causing her to be rendered in stone and paint as he
remembered her.[7] For the present purpose, it may be enough to recognize the impulse to narrative without supplying the narrative itself. But
it is necessary to see that impulse as a response to an irrepressible
liveliness which the Shakespeare monument does not share. Does that
make the style of Shakespeare's effigy different from Vaulx's in kind or
only in degree, and to what extent is the difference marked by differences in the form of narrative response demanded?

Certainly the Shakespeare effigy vigorously portrays a life, just as
Elizabethan portraits do. It is painted in natural hues, as was often the
later Elizabethan and Jacobean habit. Since it was painted a stone colour in the eighteenth century[8] and only later restored, its colours cannot be claimed to be absolutely authentic, but they are characteristic of
those found on other monuments from the same period. It shows a
prosperous gentleman, full-cheeked and well turned out, not so much
at the end of his life as comfortable in its dispensation. The monument
displays Shakespeare's arms, inherited (by Shakespeare's own contriv-
ance) from his father. He is a gentleman and better, he is a gentleman's
son, retired to the enjoyment of a well-merited prosperity. He wears
that gentle condition easily, because it is rightly worn, even if he had to
work to get it, but his mature face wears at best an abstracted expression. He looks into the distance, seeing we do not know what "far off
mountains turned into clouds" or seeing nothing at all. In his hands are
the tools which both earned him his place in the world and now stand
ready to record his vision. But they will not, for "Olympus has him," as
the epitaph says. Our responses, though, are less to the monument
than to the idea of the poet, gleaned elsewhere. When we come to
respond to the monument, Shakespeare's effigy appears a little wanting
in liveliness. That, however, may be the result of making a Caroline
gesture toward a piece of Elizabethan style. In other words, if we have
inspected this version of Shakespeare's face for evidence of the man, we
may have been looking in the wrong place.

To get at this difference in style and responding narrative gesture, it is useful to establish a continuum of face-related liveliness, along which to place these effigies. The portrait of Elinor Palmer attributed to Sir William Segar (1595) is an example of the high Elizabethan end of this scale (fig. 3). The face is flooded with light in the manner made popular by Hilliard, the features almost indecipherable by contrast with the costume, toward which the eye is directed. To read this lady and her place in the world, to see her in the round, we must inspect not the face at all, but the costume, just as in seeing the great portraits of Elizabeth the mind must recompose elements within the by-work to realize the figure fully.

By the time of Shakespeare's death, however, there were already hints of a changing style, even in the work of a single painter and sometimes within a single canvas. Thus, when William Larkin painted Sir Francis Bacon in 1610, he directed the eye chiefly to a well modeled face set above a slightly darkened ruff. Only the hands and the lace cuffs above them compete for attention, while the pendant Bacon wears is recessive, even set against a dark ground (fig. 4). By contrast, the portrait of Catherine, Countess of Salisbury, attributed to Larkin and thought to have been painted five or ten years later, shows only a little of the interest in the face and a great deal more in the elaborate rendering of lace and brocade characteristic of painting fifteen years earlier (fig. 5). To confuse matters further, Larkin's portrait of Anne Clifford, Countess of Dorset, which he painted at about the same time, combines the modeled face with the elaborate treatment of dress (fig. 6).

In fact it is noticeable that the men Larkin painted in the second decade of the seventeenth century tend to be rendered as Bacon was, while the costumes of the women receive far greater attention; but that is less interesting than the treatment of the face. Portrait painters must please their sitters, or else there is no work; but fashion appears to have been spreading the changed style at least as much as it continued to insist on the detailed rendering of a fine gown. In portraiture, full concentration on the face was still some distance away; even Van Dyck used emblematic objects in his portraits a decade and more later. But twenty years before the Vaulx monument was made, interest in the face was already in evidence, mixed with the older style which figured forth the sitter's attributes in his costume and accoutrements, or in the portrait's background.

In portraiture the accurate rendering of the face is among the most taxing perspective problems, exceeded in difficulty only by the rendering of the hands, and it is among the most difficult to accomplish in the absence of perspective technique. It is at the same time the most ordinary demand of a sitter, and since the 1620s in the English-speaking world it has been almost the single aspect by which the excellence of a portrait has been judged by those who commission it, or who see it when it is done. The Elizabethan taste in this matter seems to have been somewhat different and even though Elizabethans show a concern for resemblance which in principle we would find familiar, their attitude to that issue takes some unexpected turnings.

Hilliard, whose interest in rendering the features was enforced by his activity as a miniaturist, devotes considerable attention to the technical problem in *The Arte of Limning*, but even though he discusses foreshortening as well as proportion, he concentrates on "shadowing" (shading to give the effect of roundness) and colour as means of achieving the subtle plasticity often evident in the faces of his miniatures. His techniques are related always to close observation rather than a technical command of perspective drawing. The facial liveliness in some of his miniatures testifies both to the strength of his observation and his skills. It is therefore a matter of some irony that it was Hilliard's full scale portraits of Elizabeth that seem to have done most to divert Elizabethan popular taste from the face to the costume and by-work.

This appears to have happened for two convergent reasons. The first was an important technical consideration; the second was a question of public taste. Leonardo's recommendation of a clear, unshadowed and unreflected northern light was noted by Giovanni Paulo Lomazzo, whose *Trattato dell'arte della Pittura* (1584) was "Englished" by the Oxford scholar Richard Haydcocke and read by Hilliard. Hilliard seems to have given some account of this to Elizabeth on the first occasion of her sitting to a Hilliard portrait, and she may have slightly misunderstood it or its consequences. In the event, as Hilliard says, she "chosse her place to sit in for that perposse in the open ally of a goodly garden, where no tree was neere, nor anye shadowe at all."[9] This almost certainly had the effect of forcing the artist to work in a light which was "too high" (29), a thing which Hilliard came to know was problematic. The effect of this would have been to flatten the features and lessen the intensity of colour, on which the rendering of the well-modelled face depends to a considerable degree in the absence of perspective drawing.

Fashion seems to have done the rest, reinforced as Linda Bradly Salomon notes, by "Elizabeth's decision to remain forever youthful in her public presentation [which meant] that, while the ornate encrustations of her dress grow increasingly lavish at Hilliard's hand, the face becomes a bland mask with no truth in it."[10] It would be a mistake, though, to think that this was all a matter of the royal leadership of fashion; interest in surfaces was intrinsic both to the limning style (which produced work meant to be seen close up and thus in detail) and to the Elizabethan taste for the elaborated surface as a statement of public consequence or (especially later in the period) interior condition. This was one of the forces which led toward the Elizabethan idea of representation, which was linked to a clearly realized sense that portraits served a social as well as a representational purpose, and that these were intertwined matters, requiring expressions more elaborate and perhaps more specific than the face could contain.

The reduction of interest in the face at least played into, if it did not clear the way for, that engagement with the emblematic style which came to be so marked a feature of portraiture in the period. An Elizabethan sitting to a limner would have been concerned to show how he looked, of course. That interest never disappeared. But the phrase would have meant not only his likeness, but the projection of both his condition and his place in the world. It would be that figure he meant to transmit to his descendants.[11] The focus of Elizabethan painting was on the sitter in a visual context containing externalized signs of the character and the life depicted in the painting. The sitter is central to the portrait, but it is necessary to look everywhere in the painting in order to see the figure in perspective. That perspective is not spatial, which in England is the property of the later Jacobean and Caroline portrait style, but moral or historical – the sometimes graphically, sometimes enigmatically pictured layers of event in a life.

In externalizing aspects of a sitter's life and condition, this form of portraiture little regarded the ordinary unities of time and space. It did not, however, often abandon settings which suggested that those unities might still apply. The generally realistic style of these backgrounds seems to demand that their elements be related to each other in the same time and space, as visual realism requires. In fact, the primary relationship of these elements in an Elizabethan portrait is established by the sitter, and though artifacts were placed in the same setting, they could belong to different times and distant locations – the threatening arrival and shattered departure of the Armada seen from two windows of the same room as they are in the Armada portrait of Elizabeth (fig. 7) or, in the painting of Elizabeth in Procession to Blackfriars, two castles from widely separated locations set in the same landscape (fig. 8).[12] Realism – if not the rendering of actual places, then at least an orderly and plausible spatial arrangement – was a criterion for the composition but not the internal structure of the Elizabethan painting. This divergence between exterior and interior ordering principles was lost in the enormous increase in visual realism which caught the Caroline imagination. Each style called for different interpretive gestures to fufill the demand for narrative that each made.

The relationship of an interpreter to an Elizabethan painting is constrained by the elements present in it. They have been "broken out" of the figure on which the portrait centres, representing character or history by externalized and specific visual references – by a sieve, for example, or a broken Spanish man of war. This is a widespread presentational mode. It is to be seen not only in portraiture but as much in the pen and paper in the hands of Shakespeare's effigy, in the emblematic designs which influenced the style, in the theatre proper, and in tournaments and other public shows. For their part, impresas were already a part of costume, as a portrait of Sir Henry Lee shows (fig. 9), and by being borne in this fashion had come into the same relationship to their bearers as parallel elements in a portrait held to its sitter.

Confronting either the impresa-wearing Elizabethan or his portrait, the business of the observer is recomposition. This recomposing action follows a pattern in which the various elements found in the portrait are referenced in two directions: outward, toward more or less agreed meanings or to meanings which can be inferred independently; then inward to the subject. Sieves have an agreed meaning, while battered Spanish warships juxtaposed with brave new ones in what must be the same sea do not; but the interpreter extracts each of them from the matrix of the painting that contains them. The sieve is an impresa, recognizable because of its agreed meaning and isolated within the portrait because it is inappropriate in Elizabeth's hand. The ships of the Armada portrait are similarly identified as interpretively separate because their juxtaposition is improbable in the same moment and must be accounted for. They may have an emblematic meaning as ships, but their historical meaning seems to be the important one: these are the ships of the Armada as they approach England, and again as they depart, battered by English ships in the service of the queen, and by the hand of God in defence of His religion.

The reintegration of these elements to the painting is what gives the Elizabethan portrait a special kind of elaboration and enrichment, but also an especially defined and restricted interpretation. The Sieve portrait (fig. 10) depicts the queen as both pure and (as a result of her purity) wise, for as the English translation of Claude Paradin's *Heroicall Devices* (1591) says of the sieve emblem (fig. 11) "the nature of a riddle or siue doth represent the good and honest, for euery sive deuideth the good corne, and the profitable graine, from the unprofitable: so in like manner both the good and euil, haue knowledge to judge and diseerne betwixt the nature and property of things, which the wicked do not, but heape vp euerie thing without the riddle or siue of reason."[13] The Armada portrait shows her not only as queen, but also as the true defender of the faith, for whose earthly salvation God has intervened. In each case, the interpretive gesture follows a well defined, formal pattern and the resulting narrative is constrained by the use of emblematic elements or structures. The reconstructive action of the interpreter is related to puzzle solving and where meaning is uncertain, that is the result of information which is present, but disguised. If, for example, we do not understand Sir Henry Lee's portrait, that is because we have not yet identified his impresa. If we come to understand it, our understanding will be accompanied and coloured by the pleasures of discovering the symmetries of a closed economy, of reintegrating the many elements of the painting into an imaginative whole.

There is something oddly comforting and almost domestic about this constraint upon the narrative impulse, because the first text is a plan for the one derived from it, and the derived text may venture no farther than its original indicates. The mouse that gnaws within the rib cage of a monk's depicted corpse on the Wakeman cenotaph[14] in Tewkesbury Abbey may be startling or even shocking, but in another sense it comforts because it exactly limits the narrative response to a contemplation of mortality, a subject with well-understood parameters. It is Dr Vaulx's expression which transcends the routine *memento mori* on which his elbow rests and invites an interpretive gesture which is responsive to ambivalences rather than to defined structures, whether they are imposed by the formal arrangement of elements within the portraits, or the nature of the tomb which seeks with incomplete success to contain them.

The narrative which results is open-ended and speculative because Vaulx's portrait with its expressive face seems to reveal much, but in fact says little, and nothing that is specific. In this, it is wholly unlike its Elizabethan predecessors, in which faces seem to say little, but in which costume and accoutrements provide the dimensionality which drawing does not. When perspective became more exact and faces more realistically open and expressive, information became less so, which is exactly the opposite of what must have seemed the case to a period observer. The better the drawing, the more it diverted attention from the by-work in which meaning was externalized and finally, the more that by-work diminished. In its absence, an accumulated vocabulary of signs with agreed meanings would have been of little help. Instead, the interpreter of the text was thrown on his own imaginative resources for dealing with *lacunae* left by the ignored or departed by-work.

It is in those empty spaces that narrative grows, producing texts which in their liveliness oppose the formal structures that contain them. In just such a way Vaulx's name, a sombre jest in a living doctor, becomes in death a lively gesture toward life and signals the ambiguities of the monument which contains his portrait and those of his wives. The three portrait effigies of the Vaulx monument are not three separate likenesses. They are related to each other by the empty spaces between them, which are handy metaphors for ellipses in the story which the portraits seem to tell. It is those spaces toward which the reader-poet makes his interpretive gesture. He will not find there the patterns which he needs for the recomposition of the work of art, the solution of the puzzle. He will discover instead a vacancy in nature which he will be impelled to fill with a narrative meant to connect one portrait with another.

That narrative impulse does not begin, however, with the spaces themselves, but with the deceptive openness of the expressive portraits. The vaults below this monument contain only Vaulx, who are themselves vaults empty of the spirit that animated them. "None but Vaulx can lye below." But the speaking stones above are as much vault as Vaulx, although peculiarly carrying their meaning on the outside, hidden in faces full of suggestion. Those faces and gesturing hands give small guidance to the narrative responses they evoke, although they do give some. Edith Jinner's left hand (provided one supplies the missing first finger) replicates a gesture found frequently in portraits of the Virgin,[15] while on a very different and much less specific level, Vaulx's finger marks a place in his book, in the most ordinary way suggesting a man interrupted in his study, perhaps by Death himself. Largely, though, it is the faces which catch the eye, and they indicate only an imaginative direction. Then they leave us alone with ourselves.

We have been freed by the artist's freedom to judge "that which is fittest for the eye to see." He may have taken that freedom, ironically, only in order to represent better the life he saw before him: teasing out the strands of character or event in emblematic detail or foreshortening a nose and raising an eye in order to make a piece of vellum better suggest the living man or woman represented on it. Armed with imagination, Sidney's better sort of limner was the interpreter, not the transcriber of nature. The techniques which he deployed in order to do that required him to remake the object of his study, in a very literal way.

It is this which Hilliard voices as the need to falsify in order to render in two dimensions what he has seen in three. It is, as well, the starting point of Sidney's distinction between one sort of limner and another. But the imaginative liberty which Sidney extols brings a burden with it: caught between the need to render the subject and the need to falsify what is before the eye in order to do it, the limner is prey to opposing forces which separate him from his subject as he seeks to render it. As long as the limner could cling to emblematic devices and the surfaces of finely delineated costume, he could reasonably aim both to control the relationship between text and interpretation, and to limit the subsequent interpretation of his own work. But the more attention came to turn upon realistic and lively expression, the less specific guidance the work gave, and the more the interpretive gesture – the impulse toward narrative – became continuous with the act of making.

The release of interpretive response from formal constraints left the viewer in contemplation of suggestive faces and beckoning silences. The comfortable possibility of a resolved text was replaced by a narrative open-endedness which was always implicit in the recomposing action required by the earlier, emblematic style, but which now offered only the freedom to invest emptiness with meanings of his own. Interpretation, which must have seemed to become simpler because it was based on responses to facial expression rather than on the possession of relatively esoteric knowledge, became in reality far more difficult and dangerous, a model of experience much attended by imaginative uncertainty.

NOTES

1 *The Correspondence of Sir Philip Sidney and Hubert Lanquet*, ed. Steuart R. Pears, (London: William Pickering 1845), 29–30, 43, 77–8. Veronese was a master of perspective, noted for *trompe-l'oeil* effects in frescoes. The portrait was begun in Venice on 26 February 1574 (Sidney's letter suggests a three- or four-day sitting) and the completed work was in Languet's hands in Vienna by June of that year. Neither Sidney nor Languet describe it, and no known trace of it remains beyond references in the correspondence between the two men. For the Latin texts of Sidney's letters on the subject, see *The Prose Works of Sir Philip Sidney*, ed. Albert Feuillerat, 3 vols. (Cambridge: Cambridge University Press 1968), 3: 83, 87.

2 Nicholas Hilliard, "A Treatise Concerning the Arte of Limning" in *Nicholas Hilliard's Art of Limning*, ed. Arthur F. Kinney (Boston: Northeastern University Press 1983), 27. It is Hilliard who reports Sidney's question. Hil-

liard's response was directed characteristically at the observation and correct rendering of proportion, but neither here nor elsewhere does he speak about vanishing points and horizons, on which perspective depends.

3 *Elizabethan Critical Essays*, ed. G. Gregory Smith, 2 vols. (London: Oxford University Press 1969), 1: 156. All further quotations from this text.

4 S. Schoenbaum, *Shakespeare: A Documentary Life* (New York: Oxford University Press 1975), 254.

5 " 'Wilm Shakespeare 1609': the Flower Portrait Revisited" in *Shakespeare Quarterly*, 37, no. 1 (Spring, 1986): 83.

6 Good examples are shown in parenthesis. None is unique.

7 Edith Jinner's costume is middle Jacobean, but her left hand is posed in a gesture which began to have some currency in English portraiture just a little earlier, around 1605 (see note 15). Taken together, these things suggest the use of an earlier portrait dating from about 1610 or slightly later. This would not have been unprecedented. Lady Elizabeth Hoby, mother of Sir Thomas, certainly did precisely this when arranging for her monument (All Saints' Church, Bisham, Berkshire). In any case, it is hard to see what else could have been done to guide the carver, but none of these things are proof, of course.

8 R.M. Frye, "Portraits of Shakespeare" in *Shakespeare's Life and Times* (Princeton: Princeton University Press 1967), unpaginated.

9 Hilliard, "Arte of Limning" in Kinney, 29.

10 Arthur Kinney, "The Art of Nicholas Hilliard" in Kinney, *Hilliard's Art of Limning*, 81.

11 Roy Strong, *The English Icon*, (London: Routledge and Kegan Paul 1979), 38–9. Strong quotes briefly from *The Autobiography of Thomas Whythorne*, ed. J. Osborne (London: Oxford University Press 1961), 20. Whythorne sets out two reasons for having a portrait made: portraits not only show how one looks now, but serve at a later time to show how one looked before, and they may as well serve as encouragement or admonition to one's friends and children.

12 A lengthy and convincing discussion of this matter can be found in Roy Strong, *The Cult of Elizabeth* (London: Thames and Hudson 1977).

13 P.S., trans., *The Heroicall Devices of M. Claudius Paradin* (London: William Kearney 1591), 184.

14 The figure of a decaying monk which decorates the cenotaph is host not only to a mouse (in the abdomen), but a frog (left side of neck) and a beetle (left arm).

15 Edith Jinner's left hand is raised toward her right breast. The forefinger has been broken off, but inspection shows it to have been separated from

the middle fingers, as is the now broken small finger. The gesture is to be seen in the right hands of several pictures of the Virgin. Two important examples are Peragiminio's "Virgin with the Long Neck" and Durer's "Virgin Nursing her Child." The Durer shows the Virgin holding her exposed left breast between fore and middle finger in order to express the milk. The use of the left rather than the right hand in the Jinner effigy can be accounted for either by the need to make a simultaneous assertion of both a moral similarity and a practical difference between the lady and the saint, or by the carver's (or the painter of the putative earlier portrait) having worked from an engraving. On the other hand, a follower of Rogier Van der Weyden painted the Madonna ca. 1440 with an identical gesture of the left hand, suckling the infant Christ at her bared breast. Veronese used the gesture in a full scale portrait ("Unknown Lady," 1560). In England, Hilliard used what I believe is a disguised form of the gesture in the Pelican portrait of Elizabeth (1572–6); and later on Peter Oliver, who visited Venice and Milan in the middle 1590s, used versions of it several times, most notably in two miniatures of Anne of Denmark (1604 and 1605).

Figure 1
Vaulx monument, St Mary's Church, Meysey Hampton.

Figure 2
Shakespeare monument, Holy Trinity Church, Stratford.

Figure 3
Portrait of Elinor Palmer attributed to Sir William Segar.
Mrs P.A. Tritton

Figure 4
Portrait of Sir Francis Bacon by William Larkin.
Reproduced by kind permission of Sir Nicholas Bacon, Bt.

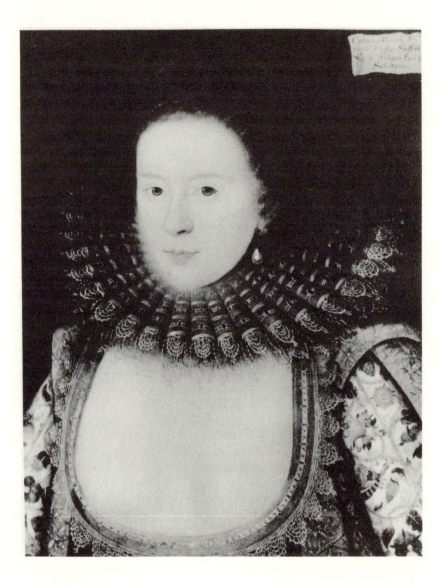

Figure 5
Portrait of Catherine, Countess of Sailsbury, attributed to William Larkin.
By kind permission of the Marquess of Tavistock, Woburn Abbey

Figure 6
Portrait of Anne Clifford, Countess of Dorset, by William Larkin.
Reproduced by courtesy of The Lord Sackville

Figure 7
Armada Portrait of Elizabeth I attributed to George Gower.
By kind permission of the Marquess of Tavistock, Woburn Abbey

OVERLEAF
Figure 8
A Procession of Elizabeth I by Robert Peake the Elder.
Private Collection

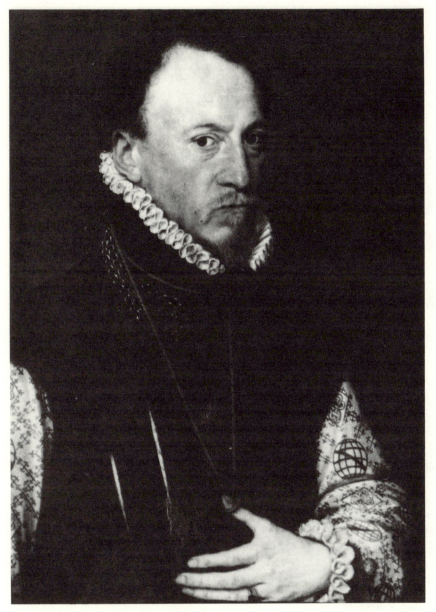

Figure 9
Portrait of Sir Henry Lee by Antonio Mor, The National Portrait Gallery.
Reproduced by kind permission of The National Portrait Gallery.

Figure 10
Sieve Portrait of Elizabeth I, Pinacoteca, Siena.
Reproduced by kind permission of the foto Soprintendenza B.A.S., Siena.

Ecquis difcernit vtrunque?

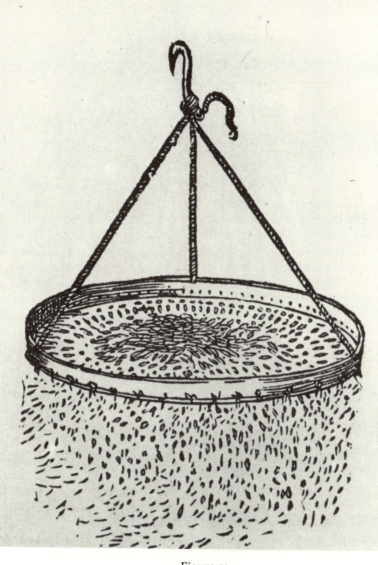

Figure 11
Sieve emblem from *Heroicall Devises*, Stirling-Maxwell Collection.
Reproduced by kind permission of the Glasgow University Library

ELAINE BANDER

Jane Austen and the Uses of Silence

When Edward Ferrars visits Barton Cottage near the end of *Sense and Sensibility*, he intends to propose to Elinor Dashwood. Nevertheless he falls into a silent reverie followed by wordless flight from Mrs Dashwood's drawing-room. "How soon he had walked himself into the proper resolution, however, how soon an opportunity of exercising it occurred, in what manner he expressed himself, and how he was received, need not be particularly told," wrote Jane Austen. "This only need be said; – that when they all sat down to table at four o'clock, about three hours after his arrival, he had secured his lady, engaged her mother's consent, and was not only in the rapturous profession of the lover, but in the reality of reason and truth, one of the happiest of men."[1] Having "particularly told" many details of their courtship, including the painful, awkward silences that have plagued these lovers, Austen now tells us quite bluntly that some words of dialogue are not for our ears – or eyes. Her characters speak, but she will not tell us what they say. For nearly four hours, therefore, a crucial emotional scene is played off the narrative stage.

On the other hand, throughout this novel Austen has frequently, meticulously, taken time to record silence. For example, when the Dashwoods first perceive Edward's approach on horseback, Elinor's feelings are too strong for words: "She saw her mother and Marianne change colour; saw them look at herself, and whisper a few sentences to each other. She would have given the world to be able to speak – ... but she had no utterance ..." (*SS* 358). This silence prevails even after Edward's arrival:

He coloured, and stammered out an unintelligible reply. Elinor's lips had moved with her mother's, ... and with a countenance meaning to be open, she sat down again and talked of the weather.

Marianne had retreated as much as possible out of sight, to conceal her distress; and Margaret ... maintained a strict silence.

When Elinor had ceased to rejoice in the dryness of the season, a very awful pause took place ...

Another pause. (SS 359)

Even after Edward assures the Dashwoods that Lucy Steele has eloped not with himself but his brother, the intensity of feeling is conveyed non-verbally: "Elinor could not speak ... He rose from his seat and walked to the window, apparently from not knowing what to do; took up a pair of scissars [sic] that lay there, and [spoiled] both them and their sheath by cutting the latter to pieces ..." (SS 360).[2]

These silences are extraordinary. Most novelists would have relished writing the emotion-laden scene in which Edward finally declares his love for Elinor. Think what Richardson, what Dickens, what Charlotte Brontë, what Trollope would have made of it! Austen, however, turns her back firmly on such promising material. Rather, she dwells in detail upon misunderstandings, awkward pauses, emotionally charged silences, speeches contemplated but withheld. She is drawn not to *éclaircissements* but confusion; not communication but its failure. She cares as much about the rhythms of speech as she does about the language. For Austen, conversations are more than strings of sentences. They also contain silence, and she presents that silence intact to her readers. Within that silence, moreover, occur crucial events, for the narrative surface of Austen's novels is preoccupied not with action but reaction: observation, reflection, judgment, resolution.

Despite the brilliance of Austen's dialogue, speech is not where such activities flourish. On the contrary, talking is discontinuous with thinking or reflecting, as Elizabeth Bennet illustrates in *Pride and Prejudice* while dancing with Darcy at the Netherfield ball. At first they are silent, apparently failing to communicate:

They stood for some time without speaking a word; and she began to imagine that their silence was to last through the two dances, and at first was resolved not to break it; till suddenly fancying that it would be the greater punishment to her partner to oblige him to talk, she made some slight observation on the dance. He replied, and was again silent. After a pause of some minutes she addressed him a second time with

"It is *your* turn to say something now, Mr Darcy." ...

"Do you talk by rule then, while you are dancing?"

"Sometimes. One must speak a little, you know. It would look odd to be entirely silent for half an hour together ..."

After further silence broken by arch conversation, Darcy, smiling, asks Elizabeth, " 'What think you of books?' " She protests:

"No – I cannot talk of books in a ball-room; my head is always full of something else."

"The *present* always occupies you in such scenes – does it?" said he, with a look of doubt.

"Yes, always," she replied, without knowing what she said, for her thoughts had wandered far from the subject ... (*PP* 91–3)

In this instance, silence is hardly less conducive to communication than conversation, because conversation interrupts thought.

In Austen's novels generally, as Lloyd Brown observed and as this scene illustrates, conversations do not necessarily lead to communication.[3] Frequently Austen's dialogues show two or more people talking at cross purposes, confusing each other deliberately or inadvertently, creating or sustaining conflicts. From Catherine Morland's " 'something very shocking indeed' " (*NA* 112) to Emma's " 'there have been matches of greater disparity,' " (*E* 342), language indeed proves ambiguous. In the pauses, however, understanding becomes possible. Silent reflection can lead to enlightenment, and a quiet girl like Fanny Price may perceive more of the truth than a chatty wit like Mary Crawford.

Given this potential for confusion and ambiguity inherent in the spoken word, it is not surprising to find that even the talkative heroines like Elizabeth Bennet and Emma Woodhouse are silent a good deal of the time.[4] In Austen's earlier novels conversations bristle with silence. She frequently introduces direct speech with such prepositional phrases as "after a short while" or "after a minute's silence," as in the following examples:

"Ah! he has got a partner, I wish he had asked *you*," said Mrs Allen; and after a short silence, she added, "he is a very agreeable young man." (*NA* 58)

After a short silence – "I hope, my Catherine, you are not getting out of humour with home because it is not so grand as Northanger." (*NA* 240–1)

Marianne was surprised and confused, yet she could not help smiling ... and, after a moment's silence, said,
   "Oh! Edward! How can you?" (*SS* 100)

"Have you," she continued, after a short silence, "ever seen Mr Willoughby since you left him at Barton?" (*SS* 211)

After a silence of several minutes he came towards her in an agitated manner, and thus began,
   "In vain have I struggled." (*PP* 189)

Then, after a short silence, he continued, "Lizzie, I bear you no ill-will ..." (*PP* 299)

In such passages Austen records not just the words but the rhythms of speech: the pauses while one character reflects upon what has been said, or considers what to say next.
   These hiatuses in the narrative dialogue usually represent an interior dialogue, for in Austen's novels the most important conversations are those which characters have with themselves. Characters incapable of sustaining interior dialogues are either benign fools like Miss Bates (whose dialogues, which are in fact monologues, are all external) or morally corrupt like Henry Crawford, who will not attend to his inner voice. When Crawford, visiting Fanny Price in Portsmouth, consults her about his tenants, she demurs:

   "I advise! – you know very well what is right."
   "Yes. When you give me your opinion, I always know what is right. Your judgment is my rule of right."
   "Oh, no! – do not say so. We have all a better guide in ourselves, if we would attend to it, than any other person can be." (*MP* 412)

Fanny knows whereof she speaks, for although she speaks very little, she carries on an almost continual dialogue with her "better guide," her conscience. Henry and Mary Crawford, brilliant talkers both, are incapable of attending to that voice within. Significantly, Mary discounts the possibility of silent prayer, while Henry would preach only to a fashionable audience. Fanny, on the other hand, isolated, passive, silent, has ample opportunity to observe and reflect, and to ponder those observations and reflections in her heart. Austen shares many such interior dialogues with readers. For instance, when Fanny agonizes over her motives for refusing to act, we eavesdrop in the little white attic: "Was she *right* in refusing what was so warmly asked, so strongly wished for? what might be so essential to a scheme on which some of those to whom she owed the greatest complaisance, had set their hearts? Was it not ill-nature – selfishness – and a fear of exposing herself? ... It would be so horrible to her to act, that she was inclined to suspect the truth and purity of her own scruples ..." (*MP* 153). That final sentence is the narrator's, summing up Fanny's self-inquisition, but the questions are Fanny's, asked of herself.

Austen's other novels, too, contain many scenes of self-examination, such as Elizabeth Bennet's review of her behaviour and belief following Darcy's letter, or Emma's great self-examination after Box Hill, or Anne Elliot's emotional temperature-taking as she renews her relationship with Captain Wentworth. In other passages, however, interior dialogues are merely implied by pauses. Readers must read between the lines.

This kind of silence, although imposed upon the text by the author, is not the same "authorial silence" Wayne Booth described in *The Rhetoric of Fiction*: "If we can imagine an *Emma* purged of the improbable wisdom of Knightley and the narrator, a novel in which the reader must infer the truth about Emma through her own beclouded vision, we will have a loose prototype for many modern novels ... [in which] the author and reader may meet, like Voltaire and God, but they do not speak."[5] An *Emma* without the narrator? Impossible! Yet Austen's earliest fictions were epistolary, modelled on Richardson's novels which silenced the authorial voice in order to allow characters to tell their own stories. Richardson, however, chafed against this self-imposed silence, intruding his voice back into his novels by way of preface, gloss, and appendix (to say nothing of his extensive correspondence with a circle of female readers and admirers). Austen, too, decided early on that she wanted a voice in her own novels. Although she began by imitating (or burlesquing) Richardson and his literary descendants such as Fanny Burney, she later discarded the epistolary mode in favour of third person narration, rewriting her first three novels to include her characteristic narrative voice. Thus *Elinor and Marianne, First Impressions*, and *Susan* – all epistolary – became *Sense and Sensibility, Pride and Prejudice*, and *Northanger Abbey*. Austen tried and rejected what Booth calls "authorial silence."

She did, however, employ another form of authorial silence: the with-

holding of dialogue. Austen could write light, bright, sparkling dialogue of the highest order, but she frequently summarizes a conversation or conveys a character's remark through indirect discourse rather
than direct speech. This tendency occurs most obviously during serious proposal scenes. Thus in *Pride and Prejudice* Austen happily records the whole " 'said he,' or ... 'said she' " of Mr Collins's comic proposal to Elizabeth and of Darcy's unsuccessful first proposal,[6] but when
Darcy proposes again, Austen provides only the "said he"; Elizabeth's
reply is summarized by the narrator: "Elizabeth ... now forced herself to
speak; and immediately, though not very fluently, gave him to understand, that her sentiments had undergone so material a change ... as to
make her receive with gratitude and pleasure, his present assurances"
(*PP* 366). The formal diction and stately periods of this speech are the
narrator's own; Elizabeth herself speaks "not very fluently," but by the
time we are privileged to hear her own words again, she has regained
fluency, a lighter, brighter fluency than the narrator's: " 'After abusing
you so abominably to your face,' " she assures Darcy, " 'I could have no
scruple in abusing you to all your relations' " (*PP* 367).

Emma's response to Mr Knightley's proposal is similarly suppressed:
"She spoke then, on being so entreated. – What did she say? – Just what
she ought, of course. A lady always does. She said enough to show
there need not be despair – and to invite him to say more himself"
(*E* 431). Emma, of course, has not always said just what a lady ought,
but in this scene – crucial for the lovers if not for the novel – readers are
given the narrator's edited version of events in which Emma is at last a
superb communicator. When responding to Mr Elton's earlier comic
proposal, however, Emma had more difficulty making herself understood. Then Austen gave Emma's full response:

She was too completely overpowered to be immediately able to reply: and
two moments of silence being ample encouragement for Mr Elton's sanguine
state of mind, he tried to take her hand again, as he joyously exclaimed –

"Charming Miss Woodhouse! allow me to interpret this interesting silence. It
confesses that you have long understood me."

"No, sir," cried Emma, "it confesses no such thing." (*E* 131)

Even Emma's silence is misinterpreted by the eager Mr Elton.[7] Nevertheless the narrator faithfully records both the silence and the words
with which Emma refuses Mr Elton, whereas Austen frequently edits,
summarizes, or suppresses dialogue in more serious, successful proposal scenes.[8]

Authorial silence, then, can be a rhetorical device which an author imposes upon the text – or upon herself – but there is another kind of silence, too: the silence of characters within the narrative. In the first case a reader, stimulated by the author's rhetoric, may infer the speech or datum which the narrator has withheld (such as the colour of Elizabeth's fine eyes, or the sum Aunt Norris gives to William Price); such silence is therefore a property of the narration of events not in themselves silent. In the latter case, however, silence is a property of the events being narrated: nothing has been said, and that non-saying is described by the narrator. In the first instance the message is silenced, whereas in the second, the message is silence.

The passage with which I began this essay is an example of the former silence. Edward Ferrars's proposal and Elinor's response occur, but readers are not "particularly told" the words they use. An earlier passage in the same novel illustrates the second type of silence. At the end of chapter 21, Lucy Steele admits she knows Edward but does not explain how or why.

Elinor heard all this with attention and surprise. "And who was this uncle? Where did he live? How came they acquainted?" She wished very much to have the subject continued, though she did not chuse to join in it herself; but nothing more of it was said, and for the first time in her life, she thought Mrs Jennings deficient either in curiosity after petty information, or in a disposition to communicate it ... But her curiosity was unavailing, for no farther notice was taken of Mr Ferrars's name by Miss Steele when alluded to, or even openly mentioned by Sir John. (*SS* 126)

As the final sentence clearly indicates, the general conversation continues off stage, as it were, while we are privileged to hear Elinor's interior dialogue: "How came they acquainted?" Her question is unspoken, and Elinor awaits an explanation which is not forthcoming until the following chapter.

In this scene, obviously, silence serves as a rather crude plot device to create suspense and to prepare for further revelations. As such it is part and parcel of the trappings Austen borrowed from Richardson and Burney. She admired Burney, but she burlesqued the convention by which one lover's behaviour is misinterpreted by the other and the lovers thus separated by a simple misunderstanding which a frank question and answer might have avoided. As a young girl Austen joked in a letter to her sister Cassandra: "Give my Love to Mary Harrison, & tell her I wish whenever she is attached to a young Man, some *respectable*

Dr Marchmont may keep them apart for five Volumes."[9] The reference is to Burney's *Camilla*, in which the hero is discouraged from courting the heroine by his well-meaning but prudent tutor, whom misleading appearances have caused to distrust Camilla's probity. In her own novels Austen preferred heroines with more spunk. Catherine Morland, maligned in her lover's eyes by the duplicity of John Thorpe, heroically races to the Tilneys' house, where her incoherent explanations are more eloquent than a finished speech: "Whatever might have been felt before her arrival, her eager declarations immediately made every look and sentence as friendly as she could desire" (*NA* 102). Marianne Dashwood, believing herself to be similarly victimized, takes the bold, unconventional, indiscreet step of initiating a correspondence with Willoughby: " 'You have perhaps been misinformed, or purposely deceived, in something concerning me,' " she writes to her former lover. " 'Tell me what it is, explain the grounds on which you acted, and I shall be satisfied, in being able to satisfy you' " (*SS* 188).

Anne Elliot, too, briefly fears that she will suffer the Burney heroine's trial of prolonged separation from her lover through casual misunderstanding. (She has of course already suffered seven years apart from him.) At the White Hart in Bath she worries lest Wentworth believe her to be engaged to her cousin, Mr Elliot, but she comforts herself with "this argument of rational dependence – 'Surely, if there be constant attachment on each side, our hearts must understand each other ere long. We are not boy and girl, to be captiously irritable, misled by every moment's inadvertance, and wantonly playing with our own happiness' " (*P* 221). With that sentence Austen rejects the old formula by which silence can spin out a plot for five volumes, for Anne and Wentworth triumph in silence. Anne does not speak up as boldly as Catherine and Marianne, but in her own gentle, genteel fashion, she makes an extraordinary effort to communicate the truth to Captain Wentworth. Their courtship and mutual understanding proceed without direct speech; he proposes in a letter and she accepts with a look. Only then do they enjoy the power of conversation.

Austen's novels contain many such "silent women" (whether motivated by feminist strategy like Ben Jonson's Epicoene or by Christian virtue like Shakespeare's Cordelia) whose silence is central to their characterization. They join a long tradition of silent women admired by patriarchal moralists. The conservative courtesy-book tradition urged young ladies to be silent. Dr Gregory, for example, appealed to his daughters: "This modesty, which I think so essential in your sex, will naturally dispose you to be rather silent in company, especially a large one. People of sense and discernment will never mistake such silence for dulness. One may take a share in conversation without uttering a syllable: the expression in the countenance shows it, and this never escapes an observing eye."[10] Certainly Fanny Price and Anne Elliot, both silent heroines who observe closely and judge wisely, exemplify this ideal silent woman, at least outwardly.

From the days of Chaucer's Wife of Bath, however (and presumably before then), women had protested against such antifeminist dicta. Alison of Bath rejected the silence imposed by patriarchal "authority" – the authorship of men: "By God, if wommen hadde writen stories / As clerkes han withinne hir oratories ...," she exclaims, claiming much as Anne Elliot would do in a different context centuries later: "Experience, thogh noon auctoritee / Were in this world, is right ynogh for me / To speke of wo ..."[11] Feminist protests were still sounding in 1700, when Lady Mary Chudleigh satirized Rev John Spring's antifeminist sermon in her poetical dialogue, *The Ladies' Defence*:

Like Mutes she Signs alone must make,
And never any Freedom take:
But still be govern'd by a Nod,
And fear her Husband as her God.
Him still must serve. Him still obey,
And nothing act and nothing say.[12]

Austen shared this contempt for those who, like Jonson's Morose, pre-ferred their women silent, yet she also admired moralists like Dr Gis-borne who warned clever women to curb their tongues.[13] Even Austen's witty, chatty heroines accept limits on their speech, at least in principle. Elizabeth Bennet states, " 'I hope I never ridicule what is wise or good' " (*PP* 57), and by the end of *Pride and Prejudice* she "... longed to observe that Mr Bingley had been a most delightful friend; so easily guided that his worth was invaluable; but she checked herself" (*PP* 371).

Emma, too, although usually remembered for speaking up when she ought to remain silent, is constantly practising self-restraint and si-lence. On Box Hill "Emma could not resist" making her hurtful remark to Miss Bates which she so bitterly regrets afterwards, but she fre-quently resists the temptation to make similar remarks which, had she spoken them, would have displayed her wit at the expense of another's feelings and her own self-esteem. Thus Emma "could have" teased Jane Fairfax about the Irish mails, "but she abstained" out of good will (*E* 298). When Harriet compares Frank Churchill to her *beau idéal* Mr

Elton, Emma restrains her indignation and remains silent (*E* 200). The most extensive illustration of Emma's ability to hold her tongue appears in chapter 14, however, when Emma meets Mrs Elton. After the first brief encounter, Emma "did not really like her," but avoids committing herself "beyond the nothing-meaning terms of being 'elegantly dressed, and very pleasing' ... As for Mr Elton ... - but no, she would not permit a hasty or a witty word from herself about his manners" (*E* 270-1). In this passage Emma's "nothing-meaning terms" of social formulae are no less a form of silence than her self-imposed restraint on the subject of Mr Elton's manners.

The second visit confirms Emma's dislike on sounder evidence. Most of the chapter is given over to a fifteen-minute monologue by Mrs Elton, occasionally interrupted either by Emma's short responses (cast frequently in indirect rather than direct speech), or by the narrator's version of Emma's silent responses (her interior dialogue). Thus: "Emma made as slight a reply as she could ... Emma was silenced ... She restrained herself ... Emma ... had nothing to say ... Emma was almost too astonished to answer ... Emma was quite at a loss" (*E* 273-8). When Mrs Elton departs, the narrator gives us Emma's eloquent internal tirade against the "Insufferable woman!" (*E* 279), but throughout Mrs Elton's visit propriety and pride silence Emma. Prompted by Mr Knightley, Emma knows what Mrs Jane West, author of a popular courtesy-book, admonished young ladies: "To say what you are certain will give unnecessary pain, is not only a breach in manners but in morals."[14] Later, on Box Hill, her casual cruelty to Miss Bates should be understood as the temporary lapse of a girl who spends many of her social hours repressing the clever, cutting words which come so easily to her.

Of all Austen's heroines, Fanny Price and Anne Elliot come closest to the ideal silent woman of the courtesy-books,[15] but *Mansfield Park* and *Persuasion* illustrate how profoundly these two heroines observe and judge their worlds from within their protective silence, and how telling their speech may become when they break that silence. In *Mansfield Park* Austen emphasizes Fanny's silence. Throughout the feverish flirtations of the excursion to Sotherton and the theatricals, Fanny is a near silent, censorious observer. The rest of the Bertrams and Crawfords take her silence for granted. Tom Bertram, when persuading Fanny to act the role of the Cottager's Wife, pleads: " 'it will not much signify if nobody hears a word you say, so you may be as creepmouse as you like, but we must have you to look at' " (*MP* 145).

Later, first Sir Thomas and then Henry Crawford try to prise words out of Fanny in violations of her privacy as shocking as any sexual violation. While examining Fanny after her refusal of Henry Crawford, Sir Thomas "... eyed her fixedly. He saw her lips formed into a *no*, though the sound was inarticulate, but her face was like scarlet" (*MP* 316). Crawford, with less delicacy, worries Fanny relentlessly over her one visible, involuntary response to his conversation: "Here Fanny, who could not but listen, involuntarily shook her head, and Crawford was instantly by her side again, intreating to know her meaning ... In vain was her 'Pray, Sir, don't - pray, Mr Crawford,' repeated twice over; and in vain did she try to move away ... but she said nothing" (*MP* 341-3).

Anne Elliot in *Persuasion* presents an even more extreme version of a silent woman whose words, when she does speak, are ignored until the novel's climax, for as Stuart Tave so eloquently observes: "One way of describing the action of *Persuasion* is to say that it begins when Anne's word has no weight and it ends when her word pierces a man's soul."[16] As many critics have commented, the novel continually thwarts direct communication between characters, particularly Anne and Wentworth, who exchange almost no words except of the most banal social formulae until after they are engaged. This extraordinary silence is due in part to the courtesy-book convention which forbade a woman to express, or indeed even to feel, love, until her lover had proposed. Fanny rightly sneers at this convention, but it was a powerful and persistent one. Thus Anne is forced to communicate her love nonverbally through looks, gestures, inflections.[17] Wentworth later writes: " 'I had not waited even these ten days, could I have read your feelings, as I think you must have penetrated mine' " (*P* 237). Anne has indeed read his feelings accurately, but she has a harder time communicating hers to him. She earns her love by acts as courageous as those by which Wentworth earns his fortune; she tells a man she loves him with neither speech nor privacy to assist her. Conventional silence forces unconventional communication.

Other courtesy-book conventions, however, employ words to impose silence. By imparting a secret in confidence, one character may silence another. Dr Gregory advised his motherless daughters: "If you have the good fortune to meet with any who deserve the name of friends, unbosom yourself to them with the most unsuspicious confidence ... But, however open you may be in talking of your own affairs, never disclose the secrets of one friend to another; these are sacred deposits, which do not belong to you, nor have you any right to make use of them."[18] Such secrets, binding the receiver to silence, feature in several of Austen's plots.

In *Sense and Sensibility* delicacy and confidentiality disrupt the normal intimacy between sisters. Elinor finds "the extraordinary silence" of Marianne and Willoughby on the subject of their apparent engagement so out of character "that a doubt sometimes entered her mind of their being really engaged, and this doubt was enough to prevent her making any inquiry of Marianne" (*SS* 71). On the other hand, Elinor is prevented from discussing her own nonengagement to Edward Ferrars because of Lucy Steele's uninvited confidence concerning *her* engagement to Edward: " 'I am sure,' said she, 'I have no doubt in the world of your faithfully keeping this secret ...' 'I certainly did not seek your confidence,' said Elinor; 'but you do me no more than justice in imagining that I may be depended on. Your secret is safe with me ...' " (*SS* 132). Silenced by this secret, Elinor can neither discuss her own affair nor defend herself against her sister's charges of coldness and complacency.

Elizabeth Bennet is also subject to secret confidences which prevent her from explaining or defending herself to her family. Darcy's revelations about Wickham alter her estimation of his character, but she cannot persuade others to share her new opinion because she cannot reveal her source. Later, following Lydia's thoughtless breaking of confidence, Elizabeth learns the truth of Darcy's behaviour from her aunt. When she thanks him for his role in Lydia's rescue, therefore, she is self-consciously breaking a confidence; later she jokes with Darcy, "what becomes of the moral, if our comfort springs from a breach of promise ...?" (*PP* 381). Fanny Price, too, is beset by secrets. She cannot defend her rejection of Crawford without betraying her cousins, nor dare she confess her own love for Edmund to her uncle. When Sir Thomas examines her: "She could say no more; her breath was almost gone ... She would rather die than own the truth ..." (*MP* 315-7).

Emma, who at first irresponsibly shared her suspicions of Jane Fairfax with Frank Churchill, later learns discretion and honour when engaged to Mr Knightley. Then she must keep Harriet's secret even at the cost of her "perfect" understanding with Mr Knightley. In a rapid interior dialogue following Knightley's declaration of love, Emma, "with all the wonderful velocity of thought, had been able ... to catch and comprehend the exact truth ..." but even in the midst of her own happiness "there was time also to rejoice that Harriet's secret had not escaped her, and to resolve that it need not and should not" (*E* 430-1). Despite all the secrets and half-truths that have led to confusion and blunders in this

novel, Emma feels the silence imposed by Harriet's secret to be a cross
she must bear; therefore when Mr Knightley tells her of Harriet's engagement, she hides her face in her workbasket lest he see "all the
exquisite feelings of delight ... which she knew she must be expressing
..." (*E* 471). The intensity of her silent relief tells how great had been the
burden of confidence: "She was in dancing, singing, exclaiming spirits;
and till she had moved about, and talked to herself, and laughed and
reflected, she could be fit for nothing rational" (*E* 475).

In *Persuasion*, Mrs Smith's crucial revelation to Anne about Mr Elliot's
true character comes about as the result of a conjugal violation of confidence between Colonel Wallis and his "silly wife" (*P* 205), and is docu-
mented by "a violation of the laws of honour," according to Anne, when
Mrs Smith shows her Mr Elliot's letter (*P* 204). Mrs Smith's double
betrayal of confidence is not essential to the plot, for Anne had already
rejected Mr Elliot in her heart, but it does suggest that the laws of
honour, if faithfully followed, could lead to silence when, morally,
speech is called for. Had Mrs Smith remained silent, she *might* have
been condemning her friend to a lifetime of forced intimacy with an
unprincipled man. Mrs Smith defends herself: "I considered your mar-
rying him as certain ... and I could no more speak the truth of him, than
if he had been your husband. My heart bled for you as I talked of
happiness" (*P* 211). Nonetheless, Anne continues to uphold the sanctity
of confidentiality in her debate with Captain Harville in the White Hart:
"We each begin probably with a little bias towards our own sex, and
upon that bias build every circumstance in favour of it which has
occurred within our own circle; many of which circumstances (perhaps
those very cases which strike us the most) may be precisely such as
cannot be brought forward without betraying a confidence, or in some
respect saying what should not be said" (*P* 234).

"Saying what should not be said" aptly describes Anne's heroic
achievement in *Persuasion*, and the moral she derives from her own case
is that with which Shakespeare's Duke of Albany closes *King Lear*:
"Speak what we feel, not what we ought to say" (V. iii. 324). Like
Cordelia, moreover, Anne is the best but least valued of three sisters;
she too is unjustly rejected by a foolish father; like Cordelia, who says
"nothing," Anne's word within her family "had no weight" (*P* 5), and
like Cordelia, she chooses silence rather than pervert language; but
whereas Cordelia's silence prompts tragedy, Anne's is comically trium-
phant.[19] For Austen, too, silence often proves more eloquent than
speech. Silence is as characteristic of Austen's novels as are the epi-
grammatical wit of the narrator or the revealing, distinctive dialogue of

her characters. Austen's silence, so often morality in action, resonates with the silent sources of morality: observation, reflection, judgment.

NOTES

1 Jane Austen, *Sense and Sensibility*, ed. R.W. Chapman, (London: Oxford University Press 1933), 361. All references to Austen's novels will be to *The Novels of Jane Austen*, ed. R.W. Chapman, 3rd ed., 5 vols. (London: Oxford University Press 1933), and will be cited parenthetically in the text using the following abbreviations: *Northanger Abbey NA; Sense and Sensibility SS; Pride and Prejudice PP; Mansfield Park MP; Emma E; Persuasion P*.

2 See Tony Tanner's comments on these scissors in his introduction to the Penguin edition of *Sense and Sensibility* (Harmondsworth: Penguin 1969), 18. Tanner also discusses Marianne's silence, the result of her refusal to speak in hackneyed language or to commit social lies, and Elinor's silent observations of others.

3 Lloyd W. Brown, *Bits of Ivory: Narrative Techniques in Jane Austen's Novels*, (Baton Rouge: Louisiana State University Press 1973), 169ff. For just one example among many, see *Emma* 65–6: Emma and Knightley's conversation about Robert Martin ends in open conflict; he is in an "angry state," she is "uncomfortable," and they share an "unpleasant silence."

4 See Sandra M. Gilbert and Susan Guber, *The Madwoman in the Attic: The Woman Writer and the Nineteenth-Century Literary Imagination* (New Haven: Yale University Press 1979), ch. 5, for an extensive discussion of the silence of Austen's heroines: "All of these girls learn the necessity of curbing their tongues ..." (160). Gilbert and Guber argue that a young girl "must learn the arts of silence either as herself a silent image invented and defined by the magic looking glass of the male-authored text, or as a silent dancer of her own woes, a dancer who enacts rather than articulates. From the abused Procne to the reclusive Lady of Shallott, therefore, women have been told that their art ... is an art of silence" (43). They also argue that Austen's "cover story of the necessity for silence and submission" hides a more subversive, feminist plot "about female assertion and expression" (154–5) – but see also Leroy W. Smith, *Jane Austen and the Drama of Women* (London: Macmillan 1983), ch. 1, for a critique of Gilbert and Guber.

5 Wayne C. Booth, *The Rhetoric of Fiction* (Chicago: University of Chicago Press 1961), 271–2.

6 *Jane Austen's Letters to her sister Cassandra and Others*, ed. R.W. Chapman, rev. ed. (London: Oxford University Press 1954), letter 76.

7 But Mr Knightley fares no better after he rebukes Emma on Box Hill: "He had misinterpreted the feelings which kept her face averted, and her tongue motionless" (375). He interprets her mortification as sullenness, to her despair. After his proposal, however, he reads Emma's silence rightly, but clearly silence is no guarantee against being misunderstood.

8 Norman Page, *The Language of Jane Austen* (Oxford: Blackwell 1972), 137. Page suggests that Austen is trying to avoid cliché'd, parodic, or lachrymose effects.

9 *Jane Austen's Letters*, letter 6.

10 John Gregory, *A Father's Legacy to His Daughters*, 15th ed. (London, 1812), 45.

11 Geoffrey Chaucer, "The Wife of Bath's Prologue," 11, 699–701; 1–3; *The Canterbury Tales*, in *A Chaucer Reader*, ed. Charles W. Dunn (New York: Harcourt, Brace 1952). Gilbert and Guber also cite the parallel between Alison and Anne; cf. *Madwoman*, 11.

12 Lady Mary Chudleigh, *The Ladies Defence* (London, 1700), cited in Margaret Kirkham, *Jane Austen, Feminism and Fiction* (New York: Methuen 1986), 9.

13 Thomas Gisborne, *An Enquiry into the Duties of the Female Sex*, 2nd ed. corr. (London, 1797), 107ff. As late as 1839, the author of an extremely popular Victorian courtesy-book points out "the uses of being silent," for "such is the importance to a woman, of knowing exactly when to cease from conversation, and when to withhold it altogether, that the silence of the female sex seems to have become proverbially synonymous with a degree of merit almost too great to be believed in as a fact." Mrs Ellis, *The Women of England: Their Social Duties, and Domestic Habits*, 3rd ed. (London: Fisher [1839]), 145.

Compare Emma's parodic imposition of ideal feminine silence upon Harriet, who "could not speak. But she was not wanted to speak. It was enough for her to feel. Emma spoke for her" (*E* 73). Emma, the frustrated author, assumes the patriarchal role of "*authority*."

14 Mrs Jane West, *Letters to a Young Lady: in which the duties and character of women are considered chiefly with a reference to prevailing opinions*, 4th ed., 3 vols. (London, 1811), 3: 43. Cited by Frank W. Bradbrook, *Jane Austen and her Predecessors* (Cambridge: Cambridge University Press 1966), Appendix 3.

15 Elinor Dashwood would seem at first to belong with Fanny and Anne as a type of Cordelia, but in fact Marianne's stubborn, embarrassing silences, her refusal to engage in polite conversation or social lies, force Elinor to pretty constant conversation, albeit of a numbing or painful quality. Here it is Marianne who plays Cordelia's role, although not for Cordelia's reasons.

16 Stuart M. Tave, *Some Words of Jane Austen* (Chicago: University of Chicago Press 1973), 256.

17 See Juliet McMaster's analysis of this non-verbal communication – and the failure of verbal communication – in *Jane Austen on Love*, ELS Monograph Series no. 13 (Victoria, BC: English Literary Studies, Dept. of English, University of Victoria 1978), ch. 2 passim. "In *Persuasion*," she writes, "there is a whole history of looks between lovers" (22). See also Marilyn Butler, *Jane Austen and the War of Ideas* (Oxford: Clarendon 1975), 283. Tony Tanner comments brilliantly on this silent courtship in *Jane Austen* (Cambridge, MA: Harvard University Press 1986), 238–44.

18 John Gregory, *A Father's Legacy*, 83–4.

19 Fanny Price also fits the paradigm as the youngest and least valued (albeit adopted) "daughter" of Sir Thomas, who banishes her after a dialogue which echoes Lear's fatal dialogue with Cordelia (*MP* 315).

Escaping the Cave: Luce Irigaray and Her Feminist Critics

Three years ago I gave my class at McGill an essay to read by Luce Irigaray translated as "When Our Lips Speak Together."[1] The essay suggests that women use the female genitals as the model for a new kind of discourse. Believing that writing is libidinal, Irigaray encourages women, on the basis of their "astonishing ... multiplicity"[2] of erogenous zones, to articulate a plural and diffuse sexuality:

Open your lips; don't open them simply. I don't open them simply. We – you/I – are neither open nor closed. We never separate simply; *a single word* cannot be pronounced, produced, uttered by our mouths. Between our lips, yours and mine, several voices, several ways of speaking resound endlessly, back and forth ... One cannot be distinguished from the other; which does not mean that they are indistinct. You don't understand a thing? No more than they understand you.

Speak, all the same. It's our good fortune that your language isn't formed of a single thread, a single strand or pattern. It comes from everywhere at once. (*TS* 209)

My class was appalled: they were sceptical of the possibility of writing from the body, and indignant about the implications of inscribing a female libido – didn't this imply that women spoke from an unchanging, eternal feminine nature? That evening I read extracts from the essay to two men friends who found it hugely entertaining and laughed a great deal.

Although I believe that my men friends' reaction was more appropriate – that Irigaray's lips are, so to speak, "tongue in cheek" – it was the judgment of my class which I found confirmed by scholars acquainted with Irigaray's work. Luce Irigaray is probably the most influential of the French "feminist" theorists on North American and English literary criticism, yet she is also the most frequently attacked.[3] While her analysis of language has inspired the excellent criticism of, for example, Mary Jacobus and Margaret Homans,[4] the assumptions behind her work with language are heavily criticized. In general she is considered to be essentialist (i.e., positing an innate female nature) and even reactionary. Her favourite strategy, employed in her first book, *Speculum of the Other Woman*,[5] of repeating male discourse in order to reveal its assumptions, is considered too close to a mere appropriation of male discourse; and when she alternates this with a deliberate imitation of the voice traditionally assigned to women, Irigaray's feminist scholars are exasperated. Her political position is considered shady and suspect: is she, wonders Toril Moi in *Sexual/Textual Politics* merely "a patriarchal wolf in sheep's clothing"?[6]

It is my contention that the criticisms levelled against Irigaray's work (which represent the feminist dissatisfaction with French theories of the feminine) have missed the point, whereas perhaps my men friends haven't. It seems to me that the problems feminist critics have with Irigaray's work are of their own making, and result from trying to force her ideas into a framework which cannot accommodate them. I would like to consider the representative comments of Ann Jones in an essay entitled "Writing The Body: Toward an Understanding of *l'Ecriture Féminine*"[7] and also some of Toril Moi's in *Sexual/Textual Politics*, in order to show first that Irigaray's advocacy of a discourse which articulates the feminine unconscious is not essentialist, as her critics claim, and second, that her repetition of male discourse (primarily that of philosophy) is not in order to appropriate it, but is an integral part of inscribing the feminine. The second project, then, is indispensable to the first.

Taking my cue from Irigaray's interpretation of Plato's allegory of the cave (which takes up a third of *Speculum of the Other Woman*), I would suggest that Irigaray has been imprisoned by her feminist critics in a cave of humanism from which she is attempting to escape. Read on the basis of certain assumptions about the nature of language and the individual, Irigaray's work makes incoherent nonsense. Because she cannot define herself within the cave in which her feminist critics are writing, but neither can she do so outside it, Irigaray is attempting to find an intermediate stage between two separately impossible speaking positions. Because she is constantly in the process of escaping from a cave from which total removal is, however, impossible, Irigaray's project is ironic. Derrida says that feminist criticism tends to "arrest the text in a certain position, thus settling on a thesis."[8] The need to settle on a thesis has caused Irigaray's feminist critics to intercept the ironic interplay in her texts, and present it as discrete statements. Irigaray has been taken too seriously; i.e., she has been taken to mean what she says, and only what she says.

The misunderstanding is partly attributable to the circumstances of translation. When I gave my class "When Our Lips Speak Together," only four other short essays were available in translation.[9] Irigaray's books, *Speculum de l'autre femme*, published in Paris in 1974, and *Ce Sexe qui n'en est pas un*, published in 1977 (from which the essays were taken), were not translated until 1985, a lapse of ten years for the major work.[10] When, between 1980 and 1982, *Signs*, *Yale French Studies*, *Feminist Studies*, and *Diacritics* all put out special issues devoted to assessing the impact of the new French theories,[11] very little of Irigaray's work was available in English. Those who could not read the original were forced to rely on interpretations of its relevance to literary criticism. The little that was translated certainly seemed to support my students' and feminist critics' judgments. Yet the essays were clearly selected as most likely to appeal to the English-speaking audience at the time, probably because of their combined emphasis on the body and on language.

The essays seemed timely: feminists in North America and England were asking for what we may call an epistemological revolution, which would take place through language; feminist literary critics were interested in a theory of literature grounded in women's experience and in defining the specificity of women's writing. Irigaray's essays seemed to answer these empiricist requirements, suggesting a feminine discourse springing from women's bodies. But the essays were taken out of the context of a more complex project, and are, at least in one important respect, atypical, since they contain nothing of the interrogative method that characterizes the rest of Irigaray's work. Two of the essays, however, form part of the self-interrogation presented in her second book, *Ce Sexe qui n'en est pas un*: in the form, as Irigaray described it, of "questions ... that question themselves and answer each other" (*TS* 119). In context the translated essays form part of an interplay of voices expressing various perspectives. The book itself, moreover, has an important relation to the first book which is completely missed by the circumstances of the translation. It is intended as an explanation of *Speculum de l'autre femme*, the notorious doctoral thesis that provoked Irigaray's dismissal (with Lacan's approval) from the Ecole Freudienne in Paris and from her teaching position at Vincennes. *Ce Sexe qui n'en est pas un* is an attempt, then, to justify the first book, and even includes part of the actual defence of her thesis. Irigaray claimed that her exclusion from the Lacanian School had "played out" ... "something of this status of the feminine" (*TS* 158), which is clearly a reference to Lacan's famous statement that women are "excluded by the nature of things, which is the nature of words" (*TS* 87).[12] "The statement is clear enough," says Irigaray, "Women are in a position of exclusion" (*TS* 88). *Ce Sexe qui n'en est pas un*, from which the essays were taken, constitutes an ironic rebuttal to Lacan. Irigaray offers the lips of "When Our Lips Speak Together" as an ironic alternative to Lacan's phallus. Both, for her, are laughing matters.

In an interview for French television Irigaray declared that laughter was her first reaction to her position as a woman in relation to the dominant discourse (her position, that is, of exclusion). "Women ... begin by laughing," she added (i.e., make progress by laughter). In order, she explained, not simply to usurp what she called the "masculine monopolization of the symbolic," it is important "not to forget to laugh" (*TS* 162, 163). Although this comment is enigmatic, and needs further explanation, I would say that this is just what Irigaray's feminist critics have forgotten to do.

Irigaray's work is somewhat scandalous. On the one hand she deliberately assumes the voice, traditionally assigned to women, of illogicality and incoherence, and justifies this in terms of the female anatomy: "If anatomy is not destiny, still less can it be language," says Mary Jacobus (who nevertheless draws on Irigaray's analysis of language).[13] On the other hand, Irigaray mimics male discourse in order to expose it, sometimes merely repeating male texts in the different context of her own books. But "a woman imitating male discourse *is* just a woman speaking like a man" (*S/T P* 143), objects Toril Moi, citing Margaret Thatcher as an example. Is Irigaray, then, merely appropriating male discourse and on top of this also making the age-old suggestion that women are fundamentally (and therefore irrevocably) different? On behalf of many feminist critics, Moi asks "From which (political) position is Irigaray speaking?" (*S/T P* 142). The question, which implies "is she for us or against us?" could only be asked within a framework of humanistic feminism. The answer is that she is neither, or both.

Plato's allegory of the cave *is* for Irigaray an allegory of discourse. "For if the cave is made in the image of the world, the world ... is equally made in the image of the cave" (*S* 246). The prisoners in this cave believe that what they see on the screen, i.e., the discourse with which they represent reality to themselves, is reality. Furthermore, they believe themselves to be the authors of this representation and therefore of their own identities. "The prison that holds them," says Irigaray, "is the illusion that the evocation and the repetition (of origin) are equivalent. They sit riveted by the fascination of what they see opposite" (*S256*). "Within the existing ideology," says Catherine Belsey, "it appears 'obvious' that people are autonomous individuals, possessed of subjectivity or consciousness which is the source of their beliefs and actions," and it appears equally 'obvious' that "the individual speaker is the origin of the meaning of his or her utterance."[14] Within the cave the individual is thought to be the origin of his or her own identity, and of language. But the screen, as Irigaray points out, is an illusion which was created and set in place before the prisoners: "it is hard to decide who is weaving the web of illusion and who is caught in it" (*S264*). Because the prisoners do not recognize that what is on the screen is representation, it is for them a present, self-present reality. "Sound," says Irigaray "gives fantasies a character of pure and immediate presence that masks the artificial mechanisms" (*S264*). The search, however, for the present reality which the screen represents is futile since it always takes place within the cave. Outside it nothing can be represented – literally there *is* nothing:

But suddenly, in the name of truth, the prisoner is unchained, disenchanted, turned away from what he had considered true, from what he, and the others, had designated by the name of truth, and he is required to say what these things are that had always been behind him and of which he had previously seen only the shadows ... he has no appropriate term, no agreed-upon or suitable denomination ... Outside of language, outside of convention and communal recognition, outside of identical perception ... these things *are* for him *nothing*. (*S272*)

There is, then, ultimately no escape from the cave: "The wise man, the philosopher, will be crazy to believe that he can thus escape the uterine dwelling and leave it behind him once and for all, so as to gaze upon the earth in the open air, in the pure natural light" (*S280*).

The prisoner who, like Irigaray, is disenchanted, disillusioned, is in an impossible position: while she does not share the assumptions of the ideology inscribed by the dominant discourse, she cannot do without it. All that can be done is to challenge the inevitableness, the apparent "naturalness" (*S258*) of what takes place inside the cave by repudiating it from within. Simply to "leap to the outside" (*TS* 162) does nothing: she must be constantly in the process of escape.

Paradoxically, while Irigaray is thought to have repudiated the dominant discourse, she is judged entirely within it: Ann Jones's pioneering essay, "Writing the Body: Toward An Understanding of L'Ecriture Feminine," was first published in 1981, when very little of Irigaray's work was available in English. Jones's assessment of the French project is clearly regarded as authoritative: the essay has been republished, unchanged, in very different collections of feminist essays as recently as 1985.[15] The essay is perhaps ironically subtitled "toward an understanding," since it exhibits considerable distaste for the French concept of "*fémininité* as a bundle of Everywoman's psychosexual characteristics" (*WB* 371). It begins, however, sympathetically enough: "Briefly, French feminists in general believe that Western thought has been based on a systematic repression of women's experience. Thus their assertion of a bedrock female nature makes sense as a point from which to deconstruct language, philosophy, psychoanalysis, the social practices, and the direction of patriarchal culture as we live in and resist it" (*WB* 361). It actually makes no sense, either to the deconstructive method or to the French theories that Jones is interpreting, to posit "a bedrock female nature," since deconstruction is precisely formulated in response to a recognition that there is no present centre to a structure of meaning. Furthermore this so-called "bedrock nature" is always already denaturalized, i.e., mediated through a sign system. Since there is, says Irigaray, quoting Lacan, "no prediscursive reality. Every reality is based upon and defined by a discourse" (*TS* 88), it follows that "the sexual identity of women" is not a product of the body but of discourse itself.

When Jones castigates the French for attempting to write the body, it is she who makes of it an essentialist position, by reading it within a framework of humanistic assumptions about the individual: "[I]f one posits that female subjectivity is derived from women's physiology and bodily instincts as they affect sexual experience and the unconscious, both theoretical and practical problems can and do arise" (*WB* 362). The problems, and there are many, are the consequences of positing the unconscious as something innate and *a priori* – the strangely static origin of women's subjective identity. Jones makes of the unconscious what Irigaray (in a passage on Freud) graphically calls "catacombs" on which are erected "the edifice of his determination ... the monument of his identification" (*S* 139, 136).

Jones places the origin of subjective experience within the individual, in an unknowable physiological source: "Is it possible," she asks, "to move from that state of unconscious excitation" (which she mistakenly calls "*jouissance*") "directly to a written female text?" (*WB*, 372)[16] She then criticizes the French for a concept of femininity which "overlooks important psychosocial realities" (*WB* 369).

But the French are not at all interested in Jones's unconscious (her version of the unconscious). Irigaray would reverse Jones's order (or in Irigaray's terms, invert her hierarchy, which privileges consciousness) and say that the unconscious is not *a priori*, not the determining cause but the result of women's subjective experience. It is formulated as a result of the individual's experience of the dominant discourse – and is therefore the possibility of escape from the cave. Following Lacan, Irigaray sees the unconscious as the product of the individual's insertion into the symbolic realm (or the social values expressed in discourse). The unconscious is the language which the socialized self censors, the language which is forbidden or denied by the dominant discourse. As Anika Lemaire says in her explanation of Lacan, the child is born into "a culture which has already thought for him, but which, because of the variety of its members, does nevertheless leave him a certain margin for personal creativity."[17] It is this margin, the edge of the screen or the way out of the cave, that Irigaray wishes to locate. It is in this margin – in the difference between the self prescribed by culture and the intuition of another self – that the unconscious is created. When asked in an interview to describe the content of the feminine unconscious Irigaray retorted that it would be impossible to do "since that presupposes disconnecting the feminine from the present-day economy of the unconscious" (*TS* 124). In other words, the unconscious, in Irigaray's view, cannot be known apart from the dominant discourse (or the social values embodied in it). If the unconscious is that which is censored by the socialized self, then it is a political product as well as an individual phenomenon, and its recovery constitutes resistance to repression. Irigaray's interest in the feminine unconscious is not, then, as Jones and other feminist critics maintain, an ahistorical or an apolitical project.

The individual in this case is responsible for remaking her history by articulating her unconscious. Even Freud maintained a dynamic mutually-modifying relationship between the conscious and the unconscious. If the "child who is born into a culture which has already thought for him" is "her," she will share with other women the fact that her femininity is devalued by the dominant ideology, or to use Irigaray's repetition of Freud, she will be dependent on "a phallic super-ego that looks sternly and disdainfully on her castrated sex/organ(s)" (*S* 124). But this is not unalterable, and neither does it, as Moi claims of Irigaray's conclusions, necessarily put women in a position of despair. Although Moi's interpretation of Irigaray is more sympathetic and more sophisticated than Jones's, she ultimately takes the same position, objecting that Irigaray analyses "woman (in the singular) throughout as if 'she' were indeed a simple, unchanging unity, always confronting the same kind of monolithic patriarchal oppression" (*S/T P* 147). But though in Irigaray's view the socialized self, the women's ego, does submit to the dominant discourse, there is always, says Irigaray, something of the feminine that "resists or subsists 'beyond'" (patriarchal oppression) (*TS* 134). The margins, however, can only be discovered from the inside. When Jones says that "what we need to do is to move outside that male-centered, binary logic altogether" (*WB* 369), Irigaray considers such judgments "naive ... we do not escape so easily from reversal. We do not escape in particular by thinking we can dispense with a rigorous inter-pretation of phallocentrism. This is no simple manageable way to leap to the outside ..." (*TS* 162).

We can begin to see why Irigaray considers it necessary to repeat male texts. She goes over certain texts of Western philosophy, which she says "constitutes the discourse on discourse" (*TS* 74), and of psychoanalysis which "tells the truth about the logic of truth" (*TS* 86), in order to discover what escapes their categories. The discourse of the woman's conscious and socialized self will be that of her culture. In *Speculum of the Other Woman*, Irigaray was, she explained, "attempting to move back through the "masculine" imaginary, that is our cultural imaginary ... to allow me to situate myself with respect to it as a woman, implicated in it and at the same time exceeding its limits" (*TS* 162-3). That latency or "excess" beyond the limits of "the cultural imag-inary" is the feminine unconscious (*TS* 163).

Although this unconscious "Other" self cannot be directly articu-lated, it makes itself known by sabotaging conscious discourse. In the words of Lemaire: "At certain privileged points, such as slips of the tongue and jokes, language seems to be torn apart, to burst with a kind of madness. It then allows true speech, the unconscious, to break through, usually in a veiled and incomprehensible form" (*JL* 188). The detailed and minute repetition of the words of Freud and Plato in *Speculum* is intended to allow "true speech" to burst through. Irigaray was, she said, having "a fling with the philosophers" (*TS* 150). The humour is important.

Laughter "tears apart language" or, as Derrida says, "bursts through only on the basis of an absolute renunciation of meaning."[18] Irigaray claims that her first reaction to the texts of Western philosophy, or as Lacan would say to her exclusion from the nature of things, is always laughter. "Isn't the phallic tantamount to the seriousness of meaning?" (*TS* 163), she asks. Laughter challenges "the adequacy, the univocity, the truth ... of a discourse which claims to state its own meaning"

(*TS* 163). A discourse which takes itself seriously, which believes in its own legitimacy, is what Derrida means by logocentric. Like the screen in the cave, a univocal discourse tries to make meaning inhabit the words themselves. But this "operation of discursive logic ... in its oppositions, its schisms" is, says Irigaray, responsible for subordinating the feminine, since it creates dichotomies in which one term is always privileged (*TS* 161). Irigaray laughs, then, in order to escape from "the seriousness of meaning" of discursive logic. She tries instead to make language ironic by opening the words to the possibility of other meanings. Sometimes it's enough to repeat the words of the philosophers in a different context,[19] but more often Irigaray seeks to fill in the gaps. If Freud is phallocentric, i.e., if he defines women as a gap or a hole because of their lack of a penis, it is because he defines them within categories of thought laid out in Plato's cave:[20] he places them on the absence side of the absence/presence dichotomy, on the passive side of the active/passive dichotomy.[21] Implicit in Plato's allegory of the cave is, for Irigaray, the distinction between male and female: the cave being the womb, mere matter, which must be left behind in pursuit of the higher intelligible world (*S*279, 283). But what is overlooked in all this, says Irigaray, is the neck of the womb, the passage into or out of the cave, which makes opposition actually continuous: "the 'go-between' path that links two 'worlds,' two modes, two methods of replicating" (*S*246).

In her own prose Irigaray searches for a link between two modes of speech, two methods of replicating or representing; although the unconscious cannot be articulated except through language as we know it, it employs, she says, a different structure, a different economy, which she calls a different "syntax" (*TS* 132-34). Freud, claims Irigaray, subordinated the different syntax of his patients' unconscious language by submitting it to this theory of penis-envy (*S*139). The woman thereby "shrieks out demands too innocuous to cause alarm, that merely make people smile. Just the way one smiles at a child when he shouts aloud the mad ambitions adults keep to themselves" (*S*141). But Freud would not have denied the legitimacy of his patients' desire if he had "preferred the play, or even the clash of those two economies" or "what we are calling these two syntaxes" (*S*139). In contrast to Freud, Irigaray wishes to preserve the "double syntax (masculine-feminine)" (*TS* 132) of her patients' speech. Her own prose she says comes directly out of her practice as a psychoanalyst since the feminine may be heard "in the language women use in psychoanalysis" (*S*134): She "must learn to hear how women speak, first with an apparent mastery of intellectual discourse, sudden stammerings and silences, and then a simpler language closer to bodily sensation."[22] Faced with speaking either "intelligently as a sexualised male" or in such a way that it will be "unintelligible according to the code in force" and "likely to be labelled abnormal, even pathological" (TS 149), Irigaray does both, presenting each in ironic relation to the other. Her prose is based on the speech of the hysterical woman, which is a double-edged discourse: evidence at once of the effects of repression and resistance to it. The hysteric converts repressed desire into another language, another syntax, frequently that of body language. The major symptom of hysteria is "aphasia" or loss of the power of speech. The similarities between Irigaray's text and the discourse of Anna O (Freud's and Breuer's first case study) are remarkable.[23] The loss of mastery over discourse is, says Irigaray " a symptom – of historical repression" (S135). She goes back (in a kind of "talking cure") over her relationship with her "fathers" the philosophers in order to discover the historical origins of her hysteria.

Freud reduced women's desire to the impossible desire for the penis. Lacan transposed Freud's theory of penis-envy into the realm of language, claiming that what women lack is not the penis, but the phallus, the signifier of authority.[24] It is because of this that "there is no woman who is not excluded by the nature of things, which is the nature of words." But why are women excluded from the dominant discourse? Why is it impossible for Irigaray to situate herself in the cave?

Male discourse, says Irigaray, is "based on a model that leaves my sex aside" (TS 149) (in French the word 'sexe' refers to the genitals as well as to the generic class). Irigaray's lips are, I think, offered as an ironic alternative to Lacan's phallus; and her "lips" bear the same relation to the labia as does the phallus to the penis. The phallus, says Lacan, is not "an object ... It is even less the organ ... which it symbolizes" (TMP 79). It exists only in the symbolic realm, is a condition of language and privileged only within discourse. The phallus represents authority in the symbolic realm by virtue of the fact that it is responsible for the child's acquisition of language and social identity.[25]

Because the father intercepts and forbids the union between mother and child, the child defers immediate gratification of his needs and learns to express them in language, as desire. The father, explains Irigaray, introduces the child to the "exigencies of the symbolization of desire through language" (TS 61). Desire is prompted by lack – but the lack is the loss of the mother's body, which can never be recuperated. This universal experience of loss is, says Lacan, what is meant by

Freud's castration anxiety.[26] The little boy, however, can console himself for the loss of the mother with the fact that he has the phallus, and can identify with his father. The phallus suggests to the male child the possibility of regaining access to the mother's body: it gives him the desire to retrieve origin.[27] It functions, like the cotton-reel in Freud's "fort/da" game,[28] as an intermediary ideational object in the progression towards being able to fully symbolize (i.e., use language). The little boy, then, says Lemaire, sublimates his desire for his mother "and enters into a quest for objects which are further and further removed from the initial object of his desire" (JL 87).

The little girl, however, has no symbolic substitute for lack, nothing with which to channel her libido, so that, says Irigaray, "her amputated desires turn back on her masochistically" (S124). She is, then, culturally castrated: "Is it necessary to add, or repeat, that woman's 'improper' access to representation, her entry into a specular and speculative economy that affords her instincts no signs, no symbols or emblems, that could figure her instincts, make it impossible to work out or transpose specific representatives of her instinctual object-goals?" (S124). The little boy on the other hand is "ego-ised by his penis – since the penis is valued on the sexual market and is overrated culturally because it can be seen, specularized, and fetishized" (S68).

But the consolation of the phallus is illusory – no-one, neither male nor female, can compensate for the loss that language brings – lack is the condition of language. Furthermore, as Stephen Heath has pointed out, the relationship between the phallus and the penis is problematical – the phallus can only be a symbol, can only substitute for the penis, because the penis is something to be seen.[29] Whether women are defined by Freud's penis-envy or Lacan's lack of the phallus, they still represent absence in the absence/presence dichotomy.

Women are, says Irigaray, condemned to penis-envy or "the desire to appropriate for oneself the genital organ that has the cultural monopoly on value" (TS 87) in order to preserve the masculine "monopolization of the symbolic" (TS 162). Lacan claims that the penis was arbitrarily selected as the privileged organ because of its "rigidity": "One might say that this signifier is chosen as what stands out as most easily seized upon in the realm of sexual copulation" (TMP 82).

Irigaray replies that only a patriarchal ideology would value phallic characteristics: *"the feminine occurs only within models and laws devised by male subjects ... This model, a phallic one, shares the values promulgated by patriarchal society and culture, values inscribed in the philosophi-*

cal corpus: property, production, order, form, unity, visibility ... and erection" (*TS* 86).

The phallus has no inevitable monopolization of the symbolic realm – the father need not be the representative of Law. "What meaning could the Oedipus complex have in a symbolic system other than patriarchy?" (*TS* 73). Furthermore, if women's access to the symbolic realm is, as Irigaray says, "improper," so is men's. No one is actually at home in the symbolic realm, no one is actually there, since lack is a universal condition of language. If possession of the phallus gives the boy the illusion that he masters language and that he may be able to replace lack with presence, it is, nevertheless, an illusion: "the young child," says Lemaire "submits to symbolism as a homogeneous and all-powerful mass into which he must insert himself with no hope of gaining a total mastery of it" (*JL*68). The lips, then, are as good, or as useless, as the phallus.

The privileged signifier, which structures the symbolic realm, is arbitrary, has been selected by an ideology which favours "order, form, unity, visibility." Let us instead, says Irigaray, promote a model that is closer to the actual conditions of language and of identity: "The unity, the truth, the propriety of words comes from their lack of lips, their forgetting of lips" (*TS* 208). The advantage of lips is that they suggest continuity between inside and outside, or absence and presence. If the little girl, furthermore, recognizes herself to be castrated, and cannot adequately represent herself in language, this is a universal condition. "We haven't been taught, nor allowed, to express multiplicity," says Irigaray: "To do that is to speak improperly ... we were supposed to ... exhibit one "truth" while sensing, withholding, muffling another. Truth's other side – its complement? its remainder? – stayed hidden. Secret. Inside and outside, we were not supposed to be the same" (*TS* 210). This onus to exhibit one "truth" has produced univocity: "*one* word ... Perfectly correct, closed up tight, wrapped around its meaning. Without any opening, any fault. You/Me" (*TS* 208).

"You may," says Irigaray, "laugh"; but let us also select an alternative privileged signifier to the phallus, one which we will not be able to hierarchize and subordinate. Let us alter the values implicit in discourse by celebrating the lips, which represent multiplicity, continuity, fluidity, and above all – imperceptibility: "How can I speak to you? You remain in flux, never congealing or solidifying. What will make that current flow into words? It is multiple, devoid of causes, meanings, simple qualities ... All this remains very strange to anyone claiming to stand on solid ground" (*TS* 215).

NOTES

1 Luce Irigaray, "Quand nos lèvres se parlent", *Cahiers du GRIF*, 12. Trans. Carolyn Burke, "When Our Lips Speak Together," *Signs* 6 no. 1 (Autumn 1980): 69–79.

2 Luce Irigaray, *This Sex Which Is Not One*, trans. Catherine Porter with Carolyn Burke (New York: Cornell University Press 1985), originally published as *Ce Sexe qui n'en est pas un*, (Paris: Les Editions de Minuit 1977), 64. Hereafter cited as *TS* with page references in the text.

3 Interestingly, the critics who translated and introduced Irigaray's essays for *Signs* criticize the French project in *Feminist Studies*; see: Carolyn Burke, "Introduction to Luce Irigaray's 'When Our Lips Speak Together'," *Signs* 6 no. 1 (Autumn 1980): 66–8; "Irigaray Through the Looking Glass," *Feminist Studies* 7, no. 2 (Summer 1981): 288–306; Hélène Vivienne Wenzel "Introduction to Luce Irigaray's 'And the one doesn't stir without the other'," *Signs* 7, no. 1 (Autumn, 1981): 56–9; "The Text as Body/Politics: An Appreciation of Monique Wittig's Writings in Context," *Feminist Studies* 7, no. 2 (Summer, 1981): 264–87; Beverly Brown and Parveen Adams "The feminine body and feminist politics," *M/F* 3 (1979): 35–50; Rachel Bowlby, "The feminine female," *Social Text* 7 (Spring and Summer, 1983): 54–68; Monique Plaza, "Phallomorphic power and the psychology of 'woman'," *Ideology and Consciousness* 4 (1978).

4 Mary Jacobus "The buried letter: feminism and romanticism in *Villette*" in *Women Writing and Writing About Women*, ed. Mary Jacobus (London: Croom Helm 1979), 42–60; "The Question of Language: Men of Maxims and the 'Mill on the Floss,'" *Critical Inquiry* 8 (Winter, 1981): 209–22; Margaret Homans, "'Her Very Own Howl': The Ambiguities of Representation in Recent Women's Fiction," *Signs* 9, no. 2 (Winter 1983): 186–205.

5 Luce Irigaray, *Speculum of the Other Woman*, trans. Gillian C. Gill (New York: Cornell University Press 1985), originally published as *Speculum de l'autre femme* (Paris: Les Editions de Minuit 1974). Hereafter cited as *S* with page references in the text.

6 Toril Moi, *Sexual/Textual Politics: Feminist Literary Theory* (London and New York: Methuen, New Accents Series 1985), 146. Hereafter cited as *S/TP* with page references in the text.

7 See Ann Rosalind Jones "Writing the Body: Toward an Understanding of *L'Ecriture Feminine*" *Feminist Studies* 7, no. 2 (1981): 247–63; republished in *The New Feminist Criticism: Essays on Women, Literature and Theory*, ed. Elaine Showalter (New York: Pantheon 1985), 361–77. Hereafter cited as *WB* with page references to this reprinting in the text; *Feminist Criticism and Social Change: Sex, Class and Race in Literature and Culture*, ed. Judith Newton and

Deborah Rosenfelt (New York and London: Methuen 1985), 86–101; and a very similar article "Inscribing Feminity: French theories of the feminine," in *Making A Difference: Feminist Literary Criticism*, ed. Gayle Green and Coppélia Kahn (London: Methuen 1985), 80–112.

8 Jacques Derrida, "Choreographies," Interview with Christie V. MacDonald, *Diacritics* 12, no. 2 (Summer 1982): 66–76.

9 For "When Our Lips Speak Together" see n. 1. "Ce sexe qui n'en est pas un" translated as "This sex which is not one" and "Des Marchandises entre elles" translated as "When the goods get together," by Claudia Reedes in *New French Feminisms*, ed. Elaine Marks and Isabelle de Courtivron (Brighton: Harvester 1980), 99–106 and 107–10 respectively. See also Hélène Vivienne Wenzel, "And the one doesn't stir without the other" (translated from "Et l'une ne bouge pas sans l'autre," 1979) *Signs* 7, no. 1 (Autumn 1981): 60–7.

10 See n. 2 and n. 5.

11 *Signs* 7, no. 1 (Autumn 1981); *Signs* 6, no. 7 (Fall 1980); *Yale French Studies* 62, no. 2 (1981); *Diacritics* 5 (Winter 1975) and 12 (Summer 1982); *Feminist Studies* 7, no. 2 (Summer 1981).

12 Quoted from Jacques Lacan, *Encore*: Le Séminaire xx, 1972–3 (Paris: Seuil 1975).

13 Mary Jacobus, "Question of Language," 207.

14 Catherine Belsey, "Constructing the subject: deconstructing the text," in *Feminist Criticism and Social Change: Sex, Class and Race in Literature and Culture*, ed. Judith Newton and Deborah Rosenfelt (New York and London: Methuen 1985), 47.

15 For publication history see n. 7.

16 For an excellent account of "jouissance" which is rather different from that of Marks and Courtivron in *New French Feminisms* (n. 18, pp. 28, 95), see Lemaire, 145–50.

17 Anika Lemaire, *Jacques Lacan*, trans. David Macey (London: Routledge & Kegan Paul Ltd. 1977), 64 (first published, Belgium: Charles Denart 1970). Hereafter cited as *JL* with page references in the text.

18 Jacques Derrida, "From Restricted to General Economy: A Hegelianism Without Reserve," in *Writing and Difference*, trans. Alan Bass (Chicago: University of Chicago Press 1978), 256.

19 See "On the Index of Plato's Works: Woman," and "Une Mère de Glace," in *Speculum*, 152–9 and 168–79.

20 See, e.g., *This Sex*, 73: "So the fact that Freud – or psychoanalytic theory in general – takes sexuality as a theme, as a discursive object, has not led to an interpretation of the *sexualization of discourse* itself."

21 See "The Blind Spot of an Old Dream of Symmetry" in *Speculum*, 13–129

(woman is "a *hole* in men's signifying economy," 50).

22 Quoted by Carolyn Burke, "Report From Paris: Women's Writing and the Women's Movement," *Signs* 3, no. 4 (Summer 1978): 851–2.

23 For a fascinating account of Anna O see: Dianne Hunter, "Hysteria, Psychoanalysis, Feminism: The Case of Anna O" in *The (M)other Tongue*, ed. Shirley Nelson Garner, Claire Kahane, Madelon Sprengnether (Ithaca: Cornell University Press 1985), 89–115.

24 See Jacques Lacan, "The Meaning of the Phallus," in *Feminine Sexuality: Jacques Lacan and the école freudienne*, eds. Juliet Mitchell and Jacqueline Rose, trans. Jacqueline Rose (New York and London: W.W. Norton & Company Ltd. 1982), 74–85. Hereafter cited as *TMP* with page references in the text.

25 For an excellent account see Lemaire, ch. 7 "The role of the Oedipus in accession to the symbolic."

26 See Introduction to Lacan, *TMP*, esp. 19.

27 *Speculum*, 83: "The 'fact of castration' has to be understood as a definitive prohibition against establishing one's own economy of the desire for origin."

28 Sigmund Freud, *Beyond the Pleasure Principle*, in vol. 18 of *The Standard Edition of the Complete Psychological Works of Sigmund Freud*, 24 vols. (London: Hogarth Press 1955).

29 Stephen Heath, "Difference," *Screen* 19, no. 3 (Autumn 1978): 51–112.

DAVID WILLIAMS

From Grammar's Pan to Logic's Fire: Intentionality in Chaucer's Friar's Tale

Illic Solus Deus Intentio Mea

According to Etienne Gilson, the great medieval controversy over nominalism, which has continued in many ways down to our own day, occurred primarily because thinkers failed to keep clear the basic distinction between logic and reality.[1] Throughout the *Canterbury Tales* Chaucer betrays a fascination with logic and often makes logical concepts the vehicle of his fiction. In the Friar's Tale with its theme of "intention," he not only satirizes some of the excesses of fourteenth-century logical demonstration but, while doing so, adds his voice to the philosophical debate on the subject of cognitive intention. In fact, he seems to have developed a theory of fiction from the theories of intention current in his day.[2]

The subject of intentionality, whether in the Middle Ages, the Renaissance,[3] or today, directly addresses the subject of language itself and the question of the relation of language to the real. Chaucer's inquiry into intentionality takes many forms and is persistent throughout his poetry. In the Friar's Tale the poet poses a basic question: what is the relation between the words a speaker utters and the meaning he intends them to have? This basic query opens out in the Tale to further and finer interrogations about the relation of language to the real. Does the intention of the speaker determine absolutely the meaning of the words, or do words have absolute meanings of their own? Can the speaker's words affect the world outside the self? Whatever the answer to the last question, do words have a necessary relation to their referents? If not, can language bring us knowledge of the real?

The main character of the Friar's Tale is a corrupt summoner who is associated throughout the narrative with intention and its function in language. He encounters and teams up with a devil in human disguise.

The summoner, far from being horrified or repulsed upon learning the identity of his companion, reacts with almost Faustian curiosity. He is particularly interested in whether devils have a determined form, or whether they can adopt any appearance which suits them. The devil explains that he is not what he seems, but, rather, that his appearance is a mask which hides his demonic form in order to permit him to achieve what he "intends": the destruction of souls. The summoner is enthusiastic because he perceives a common bond between them: just as the devil divides form from being in order to misrepresent himself, the summoner severs sign from signified in order to hide his real intention: to mislead and exploit his fellow man. In the Friar's Tale the metaphysical and the logical meet briefly in a warped alliance dividing appearance from reality.

The summoner further interrogates the devil concerning the effects of these infernal metaphysics upon earthly reality, but the devil is tired of lecturing and concludes by assuring his student that he will, by personal "experience", soon enough have sufficient knowledge of Hell's dialectics to hold a Chair in the subject. The first experience of these sworn brothers is an encounter with a carter stuck in the mud who curses his horses for their inability to pull him free:

> The feend, quod he, yow fecche, body and bones,
> As ferforthly as evere were ye foled,
> So muche wo as I have with yow tholed!
> The devel have al, bothe hors and cart and hey!   (1544-7)[4]

The summoner sees here a chance for "winning" and urges the devil to claim what has, by the carter's own words, been given to him. Surprisingly, the devil demurs, stating that he is prevented from seizing the profit promised by the words because they do not express the speaker's real intention. On a further try, the horses pull the cart free and are covered with blessings by the happy carter. The devil explains that the man spoke one thing, but thought another. Mental intention, we learn, determines meaning.

In their second adventure the pair descends upon a poor widow. The summoner, though he admits "of hire knowe I no vice" (1578), informs the widow that he has a summons for her to appear before the archdeacon to answer to "certaine thynges" (1589); to discover their nature and defend herself she must go to court the next day. However, the summoner offers to defend her from the charges he himself has fabricated, but the widow, who cannot afford the fee, twigs to the game and reacts angrily to the obvious extortion. With her refusal to pay, the summoner further accuses her of adultery and threatens to seize an object of some value which strikes his fancy – her new pan. The outraged widow curses her tormentor to hell, *"thy body and my panne also!"* (1623 emphasis added). The devil immediately inquires whether what she has just said is her real intention, and the widow replies with the important qualification that, unless he repent, she does, indeed, wish the summoner to Hell: " 'The devel,' quod she 'so fecche hym er he deye, / And panne and al, but he wol hym repente!' " (1628-9). With the summoner's bold declaration that he has no intention of repenting, the devil lays claim to him, and off to Hell he goes.

On first reading, the two episodes seem to illustrate the same idea: it is the *intention* of the speaker of words that has the power to affect the world. But each episode contains subtle differences: in the first the speaker utters words that do not express his intention (his final end: getting the cart out of the mud), and they have no direct effect, although his final intention is achieved anyway; in the second the speaker utters words which do express her intention (that unless the summoner repent he be damned) and her intention is also achieved, but, ironically, through the power of the summoner's will and intention, not her own. Because the devil knows the laws of cause and effect he can manipulate them. Asking the widow to repeat her intention, he provokes the summoner into declaring his own intention not to repent: "Nay, olde stot, that is nat myn entente" (1630). Here the devil has achieved a harmony between intention and its representation: the statement of the summoner's intentional evil and the "conditions of fact" in the world of the text which corroborate that statement.

The Friar's Tale, then, is all about intentions beginning with those of the two main characters, summoner and devil, and extending to those of their would-be victims, carter and widow. The term itself has a long history and complicated development in medieval philosophy, and the understanding of Chaucer's play on and with the term in his poetic text depends somewhat on an understanding of the various uses on which Chaucer could have drawn.[5] In several ways conflicting views of the concept of intentionality lie at the heart of the larger realist-nominalist debate in the Middle Ages, especially as it concerns the cognitive sense of intention. Just as Etienne Gilson has recognized that medieval nominalism developed out of the loss of the distinction between logical prediction and real properties, so realist philosopher Henry Babcock

Veatch locates this crucial distinction in the theory of the intentional:

For one thing, I suggest that this distinction [between the logical and the real]
may be understood in terms of the distinction between the intentional and the
nonintentional. Thus logical entities, such as concepts, propositions, and arguments, are nothing but formal signs or intentions of other things. On the other
hand, the real things of which they are thus the signs or intentions are not
themselves signs or intentions in their turn ... I suggest that the distinction
between the logical and the real may be understood in terms of the distinction
between beings of reason and real beings ... the real is to be regarded as
dependent neither in its nature nor in its being upon thought or upon the
categories or conventions of the mind.[6]

The debate about the nature of these "formal signs," which reached a
high-point in Chaucer's time, encapsulates the quarrel over universals.
The realist's position was that language, or signs, derived truth from the
truth of that which they signified: the mental concept. The concept in
turn derived its truth from the possession and re-presentation of the
being of that of which it was a concept. That is to say, the second
intention (concept) was created through the penetration of the mind by
the first intention (the form of the object). Knowledge of the object was
created *through* the concept, not by it, and represented by instrumental
signs, for instance, words. For the realist truth inheres in being only,
and its presence in thought and language is derived. St Anselm's theory
of signification, for instance, is a thoroughly metaphysical one, and his
logic is firmly rooted in ontology: "No signification is right by virtue of
any other rightness than that which remains when the signification
perishes ... Therefore, don't you see that rightness is in the signification
not because rightness begins to be when what is is signified to be or
when what-is-not is signified not to be, but because the signification is
made in accordance with a rightness which always exists?"[7]

However, for the nominalist the formal sign does not have an ontological connection with what it signifies, only a logical one and, because of
the separation between sign and signified in this theory, the status of
truth becomes purely nominal. Whereas for the realist language is es-
sentially re-presentational, making present the truth of what it signifies, for the nominalist the primacy of sign over signified leads to a view
of signification that is basically mimetic. Ockham, for instance, in illustrating his theory of conceptualization – in which universals are not real
– consistently employs analogies to art in which the creative process is
exclusively mimetic.[8]

Whereas in philosophy the subjects of *intentio* and *intentione*, cognition and will, were usually treated separately, in the Friar's Tale Chaucer introduces the two concepts of intentionality into the unifying arena of the literary text for simultaneous discussion and interaction. By combining the ideas of cognitive intuition and volitional intention Chaucer achieves a certain poetic wit as well as an ironic critique of dialectical discourse. At the same time he specifically raises the question of the relation of authorial intention to meaning. The idea of the Friar's Tale is in many ways embedded in several other tales and echoes them and their exploration of "entente." It illuminates in an important way Chaucer's "Retraction" at the end of the *Canterbury Tales*, just as it reflects back on the sense of "entente" in several individual tales.

The story of the Friar's Tale is not invented, but borrowed, as is so often the case with medieval texts, and it is in the numerous changes to earlier versions that we discover what the author considered strategic to his purpose. Established early in the oral tradition, the "devil-and-the-advocate" theme seems to have been written down first in Chaucer's time and became widespread in the fifteenth and sixteenth centuries.[9] The narrative consists in the utterance of a curse, often by a mother against her child, in which the speaker expresses irritation by consigning the source of the irritation to hell. The devil appears only to declare that because the words did not come from the heart, *ex corde*, he cannot act on them, and the victim of the curse is saved. In no extant source is the term "intention" used, but the formula that the words do not come from the heart is always used. In no other rendition of the tale does the curse include an inanimate object, much less a pan. Both changes give clues to Chaucer's intention in the writing of the Friar's Tale.

The inversion of heart and mind was common in the Middle Ages both in metaphorical discourse and in scientific. The *locus classicus* for the heart as man's centre of truth is Neoplatonism. The faculty of memory, for instance, is often located in the heart where images of the perceived world are stored up in order to be brought together to create concepts.[10] The spatial difference of the metaphorical *loci* for the cognitive faculties, heart and head, suggests centrality in the one case, extremity in the other – the middle of the thinker's body as opposed to the top – and Augustine comments on St Paul's locating of the *Verbum Dei* in the "interior man."[11] The language that is spoken "from the heart" is one which proceeds from the human spirit guided by the *Verbum Dei* and truly represents the "intention" of the speaker who has truly perceived the nature of the real and integrated it into his being. It is language not only known, but "felt," and thus it arises in the heart.

Chaucer's alteration of his source to replace reference to language coming from the heart by reference to language coming from mental intention allows him to establish the logical character of the theme he is treating. Having replaced the familiar device of the original, signified by the term *ex corde*, with the familiar logical term *per intentione*, the author can simultaneously place in the foreground dialectics and its nominalist tendencies as his theme, while establishing the realist discourse and its emphasis on rhetoric as the context in which the theme is treated.[12]

The introduction of the pan as one of the objects of intention in the tale makes possible a final irony in the treatment of the nominalist theme by inserting into its development certain grammatical ideas side by side with pertinent logical ones. What is peculiar about Chaucer's addition is that the word pan in Middle English signifies two quite different objects: "panne" as derived from French "pan," Latin "pannus," indicates a bolt of cloth or piece of cloth; "panne" as derived from Old English "panne," or "ponne," signifies a container, and as applied domestically, a pot or pan. The fact that modern editors and translators of Chaucer disagree over his intended meaning in the use of "panne" reinforces the idea that the author introduced, along with this new element in the traditional tale, a grammatical problem.[13] One of the most influential treatises of a grammatical-rhetorical nature, the pseudo-Ciceronian *Rhetorica ad Herennium*, addresses precisely this problem in its discussion of *denominatio* and *paronym*: "Metonymy (denominatio) is the figure which draws from an object closely akin or associated an expression suggesting the object meant but not called by its own name ... [This is accomplished when] content will be designated by means of container ... [or] container will be designated by means of content."[14]

The grammatical category of *denominatio* leads directly to the logical analysis of *suppositio*, a word or term which takes the place of another in a proposition or statement. The dispute in logic over *suppositio* and how it works is at the heart of the contending medieval theories of signification, and in Chaucer's own time the debate on the subject between the two Englishmen, William of Ockham and Walter Burley, raised the issue before a wide audience. The complicated subject of supposition may be briefly summarized by referring to the nature of the proposition, a form of words consisting of a subject and a predicate related through a copula: "man is an animal"; here man is the subject of which animalness is predicated. Supposition has to do with how signs signify terms in a proposition, so that we can substitute for the subject "man," a pronoun and say: "That is an animal." The pronoun then "supposits" for "man."

Ockham distinguished three kinds of supposition, each depending on the way signification took place. What he called "simple supposition" is the crucial definition, because it is here that he disagreed with the realists and set the stage for an alternate theory of language and signification. Simple supposition is, for Ockham, a term which stands for a concept (an intention) but does not "signify" it. Because for Ockham the concept as universal has no other reality than that of a term, that which stands for it cannot be a sign in the true sense, because it does not signify anything other than itself: "Simple *suppositio* is that in which the term stands for a mental content, but is not used in its significative function. For instance 'Man is a species.' The term 'man' stands for a mental content, because this content is the species; nevertheless, properly speaking, the term 'man' does not signify that mental content. Instead, this vocal sign and this mental content are only signs, one subordinate to the other, which signify the same thing."[15]

In denying to simple supposition its signifying power, not allowing the term to stand for its significate, Ockham reinforces the basic nominalist tenet that universals (concepts) have no existence outside the mind of the knower. Gordon Leff economically describes Ockham's position on this point, for if, in simple supposition, the term stands for its significate, "In that case a concept would be a real thing instead of just a concept ... The non-existence of anything else than individuals entails that simple supposition, in being of concepts, is of nothing real outside the mind. Hence it does not have real signification."[16]

The debate concerning supposition is, then, a debate about the signifying power of language and about the nature of the real. Scholastic logic of the fourteenth century dominated that debate but not to the complete exclusion of other discourses. The grammarian and the rhetorician continued to investigate the same broad question with other terms, terms which by Chaucer's time had, perhaps, in more fashionable intellectual circles, begun to sound quaint.

In Anselm's *Philosophical Fragments* as well as in the *Rhetorica ad Herennium* the grammatical function of '*denominatio*' is described in terms generally similar to the logical function of '*suppositio*.' Anselm, in describing signification through the use of "improper" words, uses the exact same example as that used in the *Rhetorica* to explain "denominatio": the container. "We often attribute a name or a verb *improperly* to some object [and do so] because that object to which the name or the verb is improperly attributed [stands in one of the following relations] to the object to which the name or the verb is *properly* attributed: It is similar to it. It is its cause, effect, genus, species, whole, or part ... It is its content or container."[17]

It is interesting and significant in relation to Chaucer's addition of "panne" that the grammatical discussion of "denominatio" and the logical discussion of *suppositio* define both as constituted by naming the container to signify the contained, or the contained to mean the container. Grammatically, Chaucer's "panne" is a paronym, an equivocation, and a *denominatio*, because the single sign can mean two different things: both of those things which it can mean are clearly containers – a length of cloth to wrap up a subject, or a pan to cook one in. The summoner is the first to mention the pan, referring to it as some valuable object the seizure of which, he hopes, will frighten the widow into paying him his extortion: "Pay me," he says, "or ... I wol bere awey thy newe panne" (1613–14). The widow herself next refers to it in a hyperbole expressing her anger when she damns the summoner, pan and all, to hell: "Unto the devel blak and rough of hewe / Yeve I thy body and my panne also!" (1622–3). The widow uses language with the natural common sense of the unschooled and has no expectation that she will by her curse be liberated of her nemesis or her pan.

The devil sees in this interesting semantic situation a possibility for real gain. Although "an instrument of God" and bound by the laws of truth, the devil is not forbidden to take advantage of the ambiguity that resides in signs. He lures the widow into repeating her words by asking her if they represent her true will: " 'The devel,' quod she, 'so fecche hym ere he deye, / And panne and al, bot he wol hym repente!' " (1628–29), and this repetition provokes the summoner, as the devil hoped it would, to express truly his intention of never repenting. Whereas the summoner has all along insisted on the nominalist position that only words count, and the devil has been obliged to respect the intention behind the words, here for the first time a true intention encounters its true signs, and the summoner is damned. The process of the deforming of the real into the logical is signified by the pan's participation in the summoner's fate.

In the process of the poem there is a movement in the text which carries the pan from its grammatical status of paronym and *denominatio* to a logical status in which it becomes in turn a name, a term, and a *suppositio*. By this device Chaucer achieves a dénouement that constitutes his critique of logic as well as his definition of authorial "intention." How Chaucer moves the "panne" from *denominatio* to *suppositio*, and then off to Hell, we shall now see.

The author of the tale, the Friar himself, is first introduced to us in the General Prologue as a "wanton and a mery," who has a familiar and convenient theory of signs: to give absolution for sins, he requires only money as the sign of true contrition. His theory is that some men are too hard-hearted to weep or pray, and therefore something as solidly substantial as silver is the best of signs. The paradox that hardness of heart itself precludes the reality of true contrition does not bother the Friar overly, since he is a kind of practical nominalist who would assert that there is no universal, or "real," sense to contrition, or sin for that matter, and all we can know is the individual's experience of it through the sign or name he gives it: "Therfore in stede of wepynge and preyeres / Men moote yeve silver to the povre freres" (231–2).

Since for the nominalist only particulars exist and universals are only names made up from knowledge of particulars, each man's understanding is his own and distinct. Even when the "name" of a universal is shared, its truth is relative, for it depends on the individual experience of the particular. The possibility of manipulating reality by manipulating its necessarily arbitrary signs permits a self-serving process of naming and renaming. In the most radical forms of nominalism genuine communication cannot occur, since signs have no necessary relation to their signified, and meaning is replaced by propaganda, truth by power. The intellectual descendant of Chaucer's Friar is that famous egg who said: "When I use a word ... it means just what I choose it to mean – neither more nor less." And when his audience objected that, perhaps, words can't be made to mean anything one wishes, he let the cat out of the bag, revealing that theories of language may have power as their goal, rather than truth: "The question is ... which is to be master, that's all."[18]

As author, the Friar intends to be master of his tale and to make language do what he wants. But as audience we soon learn, along with the chief character of the tale, that language has a way of asserting its true relation to meaning, even at the expense of authorial intention. Master Huberd, the Friar, has a very precise intention in his authorship, to provoke and humiliate the summoner, his fellow pilgrim and traditional enemy, and a genuinely corrupt figure. He therefore makes his chief character in the tale a similarly evil summoner who befriends a devil and ends up in hell. The Friar achieves this by attributing to the summoner an erroneous and self-serving theory of signification which is exposed and contradicted by the narrative in the fictional world created by the Friar, leading the condemned character to damnation. But the fictional world of the Friar, constructed to satirize the summoner, is governed by the author's own spurious and corrupt version of the same theory and its development identifies author with character, beating the Friar with his own stick. In the process of his poetic discourse, so full of considerations of the nature of "entente," the Friar's words achieve more than he intends, transcending the mastery to which he would subject them.

Huberd is a master of mimesis, a theory of art he apparently regards as fully sufficient for his authorial intention, which he achieves by creating a tale in which he places a copy of the Canterbury Summoner. Just as nominalism views the universal as a derivation of the particular, so the Friar in his nominalist theory of fiction derives the character of his tale from the particular summoner who rides beside him on the pilgrimage. But in the larger context of the *Canterbury Tales* the higher authorship of Chaucer turns the mimesis of the Friar's Tale into metonymy. Both clerics, the Friar and the Summoner, author and character, are identified with each other intellectually and morally, and the one becomes a substitute for the other.

In the first episode recounted by the Friar in his tale, the carter demonstrates both uses of the word "entente"; in the volitional sense of intention, he wishes he were out of the mud; in the cognitive sense of intention, he conceives of his horses as beings possessing will but who refuse to achieve his end. Thus the words which express his wish, or volitional "entente," are inappropriate to what the words signify and, in fact, express the opposite of what he means: "The devel have al, bothe hors and cart and hey!" (1547). To the summoner, however, the carter's words are sufficient grounds for urging the devil to seize what has been given to him. The summoner as nominalist takes words alone as constituting meaning and representing experience. But, as the devil is forced to admit, words do not create thoughts but only represent them, and misrepresentation has no authority over the real: "It is nat his entente, trust me weel," laments the devil, and when the cart is free and the curses change to blessings, he concludes: "The carl spoke oo [one] thing, but he thoghte another" (1568).

The second episode is a more complicated exploration of the concepts of intention. When the guiltless widow declares she has no money to bribe the corrupt summoner and he attempts to confiscate her pan, her concern transcends the loss of the object to a righteous indignation, and she curses him to hell, pan and all. Her understanding of the summoner is a first intention, a knowing of the way a thing "really" is, for she knows the summoner as a real, corrupt man. A second intention comes into being, expressed as a curse, when she makes of this knowledge a proposition: "The summoner is damned." She adds to this proposition what Ockham called a "syncategoremic" term, others a "denominatio": " ... and all." These are terms which, as Ockham says, signify nothing at all until added to another term.[19] "The devel," quod she, "so fecche hym er he deye,/ And panne, and al ... " (1627–8). Used in this way, the same way the carter damned his horses, "cart and hay and all," the pan, once enjoying life as a heavy skillet or a supple fabric, is now transformed through logic into a mere "suppositio" – a nominal substitution for the predicate "is damned" – for the summoner. Whereas in grammar the paronymic "panne" is used as a denomination for the summoner because it stands for the "cause" of the widow's righteous anger, our logical author, the Friar, fatally turns it into a personal supposition and makes it the container of that which it supposits. The summoner is in the pan!

But so is our nominalist author, the Friar. Fully identified throughout the Tale with the character he has created in order to condemn, the Friar has abased language to the point of absurdity. In opposition to his main character, he takes intentions alone as real. Since in his school personal suppositions are signs signifying nothing other than further signs, the pan as "suppositio" can be sent to hell, or anywhere else logic wills it. But the pan is a particular, or at least it was until its universal reality evaporated with the loss of being into sign. The Friar reveals his own corruption in demanding silver as a sign of contrition for sin, because his reasoning is that contrition and sin are merely word-concepts and signs for them do not signify anything truly: otherwise the concepts would be real. The fallacy of his theory is comically illustrated by Chaucer when he applies it to the pan: the complete absurdity of logic divorced from ontology is accomplished, and the Friar's authorial intention destroyed.

If nominalist logic tends toward a mimetic theory of language and art, does realism offer a theory that is metonymic and heuristic? Why can't we send a pan to hell by saying so, or otherwise affect real things in the world by language?

John R. Searle in his study of intentionality addresses the same subject as Chaucer in his Friar's Tale, using as his example not the pan, but that which it might contain:

Why can't we have a declaration, "I hereby fry an egg" and thereby an egg is fried? Because the capacities of representation are here exceeded. A supernatural being could do this because such a being could intentionally bring states of affairs about solely by representing them as having been brought about. We can't do that. But we do have a humbler, though still god-like, form of word magic: we can agree in advance that certain kinds of speech acts can bring about states of affairs by representing them as having been brought about.[20]

Searle, like other speech-act theorists, uses to discuss intentionality the concept of "direction of fit" in which we are able to analyze and distinguish intentions, as well as their representations, by how they are directed toward the world of phenomenal reality. Thus assertives are statements or representations which match the way things are in the world and so represent them; directives do not match any state of affairs in the world, but rather are meant to bring about in the world a state of affairs which does not exist, simply by representing it as existing. Assertive intentional representations have what is called a "word-to-world" direction of fit because the word "fits" the world; directives have a "world-to-word" direction of fit because the world is meant to fit, or comply with, what is said about it.

According to this paradigm both the widow's intention and that of the carter have world-to-word directions of fit since, as curses, they are directives representing states which the speakers want to exist. In the one case the speaker misrepresents his world-to-word intention, but it is fulfilled anyway. Wishing the world were such that he was out of the mud, he attempts to bring it about by cursing the means which have failed him; in the other, the speaker correctly represents her world-to-word intention, and it, too, comes about. But while the Friar tries to prove through his authorship that any sign will do, even in world-to-word significations, Chaucer, through his greater authorship, demonstrates just the opposite. As Searle says, the human mind has certain truth requirements which insist that things which happen must happen for a reason:

Now when it comes to forming concepts for describing these basic Intentional relations ... we require more for the application of the concept than just that there be a correct match between Intentional content and the state of affairs that it causes or that causes it. We make the further requirement which philosophers have expressed by saying the match must come about "in the right way." But why do we make this requirement and what is it exactly? We make the requirement because we want our concepts to express the condition that the Intentionality in action and perception must really work; thus we insist that Intentionality must not be epiphenomenal.[21]

The fulfillment of the intentions of both the carter and the widow are epiphenomenal in the sense that they are not the cause of the events they address, but rather coincidental to them; the cart is freed of the mud because the horses pull harder, not because of the curse; and the summoner goes to hell, not by the widow's intention, but because of his own intentional evil: repentance "is nat myn entente" declares the summoner and to hell he goes. But what about the pan?

The pan goes to hell as an ironic concession and final condemnation of the authorship of the Friar who represents the world as an entire construct of epiphenomena in which the world always can be made to fit the word because it is nothing but words. The Friar is the other side of the summoner's coin, the character divorcing words from intentions, the author divorcing intentions from reality. But the requirement which Searle describes, that things must happen "in the right way," and Anselm described a thousand years earlier as "the truth which is in the existence of things," reasserts itself through our perception of the absurdity and irony of things happening for the wrong reasons, and the Friar, along with his summoner, gets fried in his own pan!

Chaucer's use of the philosophical concept of intention in the Friar's Tale lends to that text its theme and structure, but it also sets the stage for a further development of the idea toward a more purely poetic theory of signification. That extension we see in the "Retraction" at the end of the *Canterbury Tales*, particularly in the discussion of authorial intention. Chaucer appears to make a distinction between his intention as communicated to his audience and the representation of that intention. This is a distinction which Searle also makes, providing useful insight into modes of signification: "Characteristically a man who makes a statement both intends to represent some fact or state of affairs and intends to communicate this representation to his hearers. But his representing intention is not the same as his communication intention."[22]

The communicating intention and how it functions has already been set out by Chaucer in the Friar's Tale and all the other stories recounted in the *Canterbury Tales*, for the text is constructed by a series of pilgrims telling stories to their fellow pilgrims. The frame structure of the *Canter-*

bury Tales is not simply the device of a story-within-a-story, but also an audience-author relation within an audience-author relation. By observing the communication between a fictional author and his fictional audience, we as "real" audience may find a paradigm for our relation to our author. Through such a device the very idea of fiction becomes a subject of the text raised repeatedly through the failure of a series of authors to achieve exactly their intentions in their tales. In the case of the Friar (and several other pilgrim authors), his communicational intention presents one thing, a nominal world, but the representational intention controlled by Chaucer presents its contradiction, a world in which the signified escapes false signs and reasserts an ontology of realism.

What, then, is Chaucer's intention? It is presumably not of the same order as that of the nominalist Friar for whom fiction is the imitation of a world of verbal constructs in an endlessly self-referential communication. Linking his intention to the words of St Paul to the effect that all writing is inspired by God, Chaucer forcefully suggests a theory of language and of fiction that is realist in direction:

Now preye I to hem alle that herkne this litel tretys or rede, that if ther be any thyng in it that liketh hem, that therof they thanken oure Lord Jhesu Crist, of whom procedeth al wit and al goodnesse./ And if ther be any thyng that displese hem, I prey hem also that they arrette it to the defaute of myn unkonnynge, and nat to my wyl, that wolde ful fayn have seyd bettre if I hadde had konnynge./ For oure book seith, "Al that is writen is writen for oure doctrine," and that is myn entente. 1081-3.

On the basis of imperfect intellect, or "unkonnynge" as he calls it, Chaucer goes on to "retract" several of the works in his corpus, including the Tales of Canterbury which he is in the very act of disseminating. The paradox of an author denying what he is simultaneously saying, or unwriting what he is writing, suggests in the Chaucerian context a realist theory of fiction in which two intentions are operating at the same time – an intentional representation and a communicating one – the one put forward, the other withdrawn. But the relation of these directions is binary, like the ontological relation of universal to particular, and as poetics it suggests a theory of fiction, primarily representational, in which the intention to communicate is variously absent and present. In this way intention itself becomes poetic theory.

The Scholastics identified intentions as "beings of reason" and described their function as representing, or "making manifest" being itself. Because of this function these "beings of reason," or intentions, are also called formal signs. For the realist the cause of their being is the "real" being of that which they mean, or show forth and represent. If, when Chaucer speaks of his intention in his writing, he is understood to mean fiction itself – and that is clearly what he means in the retraction – then fiction is conceived as a formal sign. Contextualizing fiction in the Pauline text of II Tim. iii, 16, Chaucer suggests that writing as fiction becomes a formal sign and representation of the real.

What writing, including fiction, represents through language is not, then, mimesis of the phenomenal world, for the world as the subject of fiction is itself a sign, and, as Veatch and others demonstrate, what is signified by the formal sign can never itself be a sign: "The real things of which they [formal signs] are thus the signs or intentions are not themselves signs or intentions in their turn."[23] While language is always a sign of a sign – an artificial sign – fiction is declaratory and heuristic, making exist what it represents. In realist logic a concept as a formal sign takes its being from the being which is in real things; if, for Chaucer, fiction is different from logic, which it surely is, and yet analogous to it in the idea of formal sign, where does fiction derive its being?

St Anselm asserted that the truth that is in being is derived from the Supreme Truth. Before him St Paul, quoted by Chaucer, stated that all writing is derived from God. Fiction, in Chaucer's view, is, like being, derived from Truth and has ultimately a heuristic dynamic and two simultaneous directions of fit, like the word magic, almost god-like, that Searle describes. Fiction imitates the Truth in a word-to-world direction of fit and represents the Truth and makes it be in a world-to-word direction of fit. Such a scheme with its two directions of fit suggests "another world" mediated by fiction in the real world. Fictional writing functions mimetically *vis-à-vis* the "other world" from which it takes its being, and representationally *vis-à-vis* the real world, making the one exist in the other. The paradigm for such a theory of fiction is the Neoplatonic, realist model of being and cognition in which universals (other world) inform the beings of particulars (this world) and the being of particulars creates signs of itself.

The ethos of such a system is allegory. What begins as metonymy, saying one thing to mean another, is fulfilled in allegory through a progression of signs "translated" into a conceptual language. This translation is a transference ([trans]fero, -tuli, -latus) from one (thing) to (an)other and is paradigmatic of Neoplatonic metaphysics. But Chaucer, allegorist though he was, is not simply writing allegories. By invoking the model of realist ontology to develop a theory of fiction, he makes fiction itself, and all writing, an allegorical process. And as fiction is seen in analogy to metaphysics, so in the extension of the analogy allegory becomes a metaphysical principle.

Seen in this light Chaucer's Friar's Tale provides an opening into the multiple idea of intention which underlies a concept of signification in fiction. Chaucer's intention, openly declared at the end of the *Canterbury Tales*, has been to represent the truth in his writing of fiction. What is retracted at the end is the mimetic and fictive communication which is simultaneously and continually retracted in every act of writing, in order to let stand in its place the heuristic representation of the truth that is in being. This protraction-retraction that characterizes all writing is first in the movement of the author's pen forward and backward across the paper and continues in the text's heuresis-mimesis in which representation creates and communication returns the sign of that representation to the audience. The same protraction-retraction is present outside of fiction in the emanation of being into form, universal into particular, and the return by the particular in the form of signs of the truth to being.

Chaucer's invocation of St Paul to explain his authorial "entente" establishes the beginnings of a realist theory of fiction in which language and signification – "al that is writen" – exists to be taught, disputed, interpreted, and restated in a search, not for power, but for truth.

NOTES

1 Etienne Gilson, *The Unity of Philosophical Experience* (New York: Charles Scribner's and Sons 1937). See particularly chapter 1.
2 See also Robert B. Burlin, *Chaucerian Fiction* (Princeton, NJ: Princeton University Press 1977).
3 As Professor Malloch has pointed out, the heated debate in Renaissance England over the moral probity of making a statement with a mental reservation, which alters its meaning unbeknownst to the listener, is based on the relation of intention to speech. In this sense the equivocation controversy of this later period is a continuation of the scholastic debate between logic and metaphysics and, more generally, a continuation of the nominalist-realist struggle of even earlier origin. Malloch, describing the sixteenth-century theologian Thomas Sanchez whose work was condemned by Pope Innocent IX, makes of Sanchez a worthy descendant of Chaucer's Friar: "For Sanchez words uttered mean what they say, but

the relation of the words uttered to the mind of the speaker is tenuous. He argues that external words are related *mere materialiter* to the nature of a lie: the fact that they do not adequately render the *intentio* of the speaker does not make them a lie, nor does the fact that they are not ambiguous in any usual sense, for the quality of being usual, or unusual, has only an accidental relation to the nature of a lie. For Sanchez *intentio* is all." A.E. Malloch, "Equivocation: A Circuit of Reasons," in *Familiar Colloquy: Essays Presented to Arthur Edward Barker*, ed. Patricia Bruckmann (Ottawa: Oberon Press 1978), 37.

4 All quotations of Geoffrey Chaucer are *The Works of Geoffrey Chaucer*, F.N. Robinson, ed., 2nd ed. (Boston: Houghton Mifflin 1957).

5 Scholasticism is well known for its effusion of terminology and the consequent complexity of much of its discourse. In order to minimize this complexity, the various senses of *intention* and the concepts to which the word was related should be distinguished. The use of the term intention in medieval philosophy became current with Avicenna (980–1037) and possessed two distinct meanings, one – *intentio* – having to do with the faculty of intellect, the other – *intentione* – having to do with the faculty of will. Cognitive intention describes two things: the real nature of things which may be known, as well as how the mind gets to know what it knows, and how such knowledge exists in the mind. Thus the term was subdivided into two distinct senses, first intentions and second intentions. First intentions are always about things as they really exist outside the mind, their being and their essence. So a term of first intention, let us say "man," would be the subject of such sciences as metaphysics, physics, ethics, politics, and so on. Second intentions are always about things as they exist in the mind only; that is to say, second intentions are concepts and concern mental realities and what we do with them. What is done with mental realities principally is signification, and thus as expressed in propositions, second intentions are the subject of logic.

6 Henry Babcock Veatch, *Intentional Logic* (New Haven: Yale University Press 1970), 16.

7 Anselm, "On Truth," in *Anselm of Canterbury*, ed. and trans., Jasper Hopkins and Herbert Richardson, 4 vols., (Toronto and New York: The Edwin Mellon Press 1976), 2: 101.

8 See, for example, Ockham *Ordinatio*, D.ii, Q. viii, prima redactio, in Philoteus Boehner, OFM, *Ockham. Philosophical Writings* (Toronto and New York: Thomas Nelson and Sons 1957), 41.

9 See, among other studies of analogues, Archer Taylor, "The Devil and the Advocate," *Publications of the Modern Language Association* 36 (1921), 35–59.

10 "When thou conceivest a word which thou mayest utter ... thou meanest

to utter a thing, and the very conception of the thing is already a word in thy heart: it has not yet come forth, but it is already born in the heart, and is waiting to come forth." *Lectures or Tractates on the Gospel According to Saint John*, trans. Rev. John Gibb (vols. 10, 11), 10:203, of *Augustine: The Works*, ed. Marcus Dods, 15 vols. (Edinburgh: Clark 1872–88). See also Augustine's *De Continentia*, chapter 1 and chapter 24. The heart as the locus of intention is expressed, for instance, by the anonymous, four-teenth-century author of *The Cloud of Unknowing*: "God unto whom alle hertes ben open, and unto whom alle wille spekith, and unto whom no prive thing is hid: I beseche thee so for to clense the entent of myn hert ..." in P. Hodgson, ed., *The Cloud of Unknowing* and and *Book of Privy Counselling*, Early English Texts Society, Original Series (London: Oxford University Press 1944), 2.

11 Augustine, *De Vera Religione* in *Augustine: Earlier Works*, vol. 6 in Library of Christian Classics, ed. and trans. John H.S. Burleigh (London and Philadelphia: SCM Press 1953), 262–3.

12 Holly Wallace Boucher in an interesting recent article on the influence of nominalism on Chaucer seems not to take account of Chaucer's parodying of that theory by personifying it through clearly reprehensible characters. "Nominalism: The Difference for Chaucer and Boccaccio," *Chaucer Review* 20, no. 3 (1986): 213–20.

13 For instance, in his edition Robert A. Pratt, *The Tales of Canterbury* (Boston: Houghton Mifflin 1974) glosses "panne" as "cloth; garment," p. 293; the majority of editors give "pan" as the meaning of the word.

14 *Ad Herennium*, 4.22.43, in *Cicero. Ad C. Herennium, De Ratione Dicendi* (Rhetorica Ad Herennium) trans. Henry Caplan, Loeb Classical Library (London and Cambridge, MA, 1954), 335, 337. Desmond Paul Henry in his study of Anselm's logic comments on the same subject: "We know that Lanfranc lectured on the pseudo-Ciceronian *Rhetorica ad Herenium*; this work defines *denominatio* (which includes paronymous name-transference, cf. 3.123) as a means whereby we may gather a reference to some thing without use of the word primarily applicable to that thing ... Oblique reference to the container by mentioning the contained, or to the contained by mentioning the container, is given by this same *Rhetorica* as an example of *denominatio*, and this instance is repeated in Anselm's schedule of 'improper' word-uses." See *The Logic of Saint Anselm* (Oxford: Oxford University Press 1967), 8–9.

15 Ockham, *Summa totius logicae*, 1, c.lxiii, in Boehner, 66–7.

16 Gordon Leff, *William of Ockham: The Metamorphosis of Scholastic Discourse* (Manchester: Manchester University Press 1975), 134; see also S.F. Brown,

"Walter Burleigh's Treatise *de suppositionibus* and its Influence on William of Ockham," *Franciscan Studies* 32 (1972): 15–64.

17 Anselm. *Philosophical Fragments* in *Anselm of Canterbury*, 2: 17.
18 *The Annotated Alice*, Introd. and Notes by Martin Gardner (New York and Scarborough, ON: New American Library 1960), 269. It is interesting that the annotation to these lines identifies Humpty Dumpty with William of Ockham and logical empiricism.
19 Ockham, *Summa totius logicae*, 1.2, in Boehner, 51.
20 John R. Searle. *Intentionality: An Essay in the Philosophy of Mind* (Cambridge: Cambridge University Press 1984), 176.
21 Ibid., 139–40.
22 Ibid., 165.
23 Veatch, *Intentional Logic*, 16.

Boethius, the Liberal Arts, and Early Medieval Political Theory

The seven liberal arts were an established pattern by the time Alcuin of York (c. 732–804) had set up Charlemagne's Palace School. The division into the quadrivium (arithmetic, music, geometry, and astronomy) and the trivium (grammar, rhetoric, and dialectic) are familiar aspects of the medieval approach to learning. It is sometimes assumed that medieval education was designed solely for religious needs and was thus intended to prepare one for life in the Church. Less often is it recognized that training was also required for secular administration, though recent studies do suggest the extent to which some early medieval jurisdictions relied on a corps of trained people.[1]

Once we accept the notion that education prepared students for practical careers in government as well as aiding in the salvation of souls, we want to know how the curriculum could have been designed for such formation. What was it about the liberal arts that made them apt subjects for governors and magistrates to learn? The answer this essay will suggest is that as well as purporting to teach a body of knowledge the arts also offered a training in ethics which included a sense of both private and public action. Not only was the subject matter of the arts useful and grounded in reason, but the arts themselves also offered models of ethics and justice. Our primary interest here will be with the second aspect.

The linking of the arts with ethics and justice was nothing new in the early Middle Ages, but can be traced back to a tradition stemming from Pythagoras and forming a part of the thought of Plato and Aristotle. This tradition is synthesized in Cicero's *De re publica* and *De legibus*, from which there is a clear flow to Augustine. Another important figure in this tradition is Boethius, since it is largely to him that the medieval

West owes the preservation and transmission of Greek philosophy.[2] I want chiefly to concentrate on Boethius, and on his treatises on arithmetic and music and the work on geometry which has been attributed to him. Boethius was best known in the Middle Ages for his *De consolatione philosophiae*, a work which shows the application of a system of reasoning to solving the ethical problem of the breakdown between ideal and practice, but the elements of the ideal can be seen being built up in his writings on the arts.[3]

Early medieval thinkers seem simply to have grafted the arts onto the body of Christian thought. An eighth- or ninth-century example will show how the idea was taken. In the preface to a treatise on music which lies among the *dubia* and *spuria* of Bede in the *Patrologia Latina*, there is a passage which describes how God has revealed the arts to philosophers, thereby helping fallen human nature to a better condition by opposing wisdom to ignorance, virtue to moral failing, eloquence to inarticulateness, and sufficiency to want, thus compensating for four major impediments which have entangled humanity ever since the Fall. Clearly the arts are described in terms of redemption, but this has a social as well as a private aspect. For, while wisdom may be internal, it was widely accepted as a necessary part of kingship. Moral virtue may also be private, but equally it relates to the kinds of laws a nation makes. Eloquence is public, since it refers to communication and persuasion; and sufficiency speaks not only to one's own ability to provide for oneself, but also to the economic life of a community. There is in fact nothing strange about this idea, given Christianity's concern not only for the welfare of individual souls but also for the community, the Church.[4]

In classical and early medieval philosophy, political theory is dependent on cosmology. Boethius's cosmology proceeds along lines which develop from classical thought but are also consistent with Christianity. First, the universe is conceived as originating in unity, so that the diversity and inequality of the visible world all have their source in a primal equality (*Inst. arithm.* I. 32, p. 66).[5] This equality is first patterned as an exemplar in the mind of God, and the pattern is exhibited as number, which provides the structural principle for the world: "It is from this numerical model that the diverse things constructed of the four elements derive, and from the same model that we get the alterations of the seasons, the motions of the stars, and the revolution of the heavens" (*Inst. arithm.* I. 2, p. 12).[6] The visible universe, then, opens out from its original wholeness and arranges itself in a variety of ways. What had been immaterial is now reflected in matter, and what was at rest now takes on motion. Matter can be measured and motion can be studied, so that what was originally beyond comprehension can now be defined.

Just as unity engenders diversity, so diversity points back towards unity, the stream providing evidence of its source: "Everything that comes into being out of contraries is joined and put together by a kind of harmony. For harmony is the uniting of many things and the common accord of what is at variance" (*Inst. arithm.* II. 33, p. 126).[7] This means that there ought to be an agreement between diversity and unity, and a consistency among all things, since all are part of the whole. However, the interrelation may break down, in which case one is faced with a split not merely between unity and diversity, but between good (which is the moral aspect of primal unity) and evil (which is the absence of that unity, and thus of the harmony which binds things together): "It is related to no basic principle of its own, but its nature constantly causes it to wander beyond the boundary of the original good" (*Inst. arithm.* I. 32, p. 66).[8]

Cosmic morality is reflected in the life of the individual, for the mind may know and imitate the Good, and thus it can establish harmony among the parts of the soul. The imagery used shows how in the tradition of Plato what may be said of the individual can also be said of the state: "Like a guide and leader, the mind, invigorated by pure knowledge, holds in check excessive greed and the immoderate unbridled impetuosity of rage. In a certain way it takes these forms of inequality and establishes them in a tempered state of goodness" (*Inst. arithm.* I. 32, p. 66).[9] Study of the arts is the means by which the mind attains this pure knowledge: "The quadrivium provides a way by which the superior mind journeys from the dimension of our physical senses and is brought to greater certainty of understanding" (*Inst. arithm.* I. 1, p. 9f).[10]

The quadrivium is not a random or arbitrary set of disciplines (they are called the "mathematical arts" from the Greek *mathematikos*, "fond of learning"). Rather, it provides a precise and systematic way of perceiving within visible objects the nature of the Prime Essence. First one separates the accidental from the essential. An accident is something which may attach itself to an object, but which is not a necessary part of that object's genus and species, and may change according to time and place. Essences then divide into two basic classes, multitudes and magnitudes, and there is a further classification into mobile and immobile, which thus gives four basic divisions of essences. This is the rationale of the quadrivium.[11]

Arithmetic deals with immobile multitudes, since its subject is numbers in static relation. Music deals with mobile multitudes, since it, too, is founded on number, but these numbers are in proportionally changing relationship with each other. Geometry deals with immobile magnitudes, i.e., shapes and figures; and its basic elements are the point (which is something with no parts, the spatial equivalent of unity) and the line (which is length without width and is bounded by points). Astronomy studies mobile magnitudes, i.e., physical bodies in motion (this entire schema is set forth in *Inst. arithm*. I. 1). Because number is the principle by which the universe is constructed, and because all the arts contain number, arithmetic is preeminent, and its own first principle is unity: "The first number is two, since one (as arithmeticians declare) is not a number but the source and origin of numbers" (*Ars geometr.*, p. 397f).[12] The number one thus generates a multitude of numbers, just as cosmic unity generates the diversity of creation. The relationships are analogous: "These of course are contraries. Nevertheless, they are mingled in a certain friendship and kindred, and produce a single body of number by means of the image and governance of that unity" (*Inst. arithm*. II. 32, p. 125).[13] So the tempering of the four elements and the reciprocal co-operation of the seasons, all brought through harmony into the body of one world and one year, are similar to the ordering of all numbers by one.

The arts are all interconnected. What the mind perceives through arithmetic, the eye sees through geometry and astronomy and the ear hears through music. In a way the differences among the arts are marked by nothing more than the fact that they represent the manner in which various senses apprehend essential reality. The nature of the subject depends upon the sense (the information given depends upon the nature of the observation), but the mind is in all, since what makes each an art is the fact that it is concerned to investigate the numerical relationships of things.

Just as arithmetic takes precedence over music, since the former contemplates numerical relationships with the mind alone while the latter contemplates them as they are invested in air, so geometry takes precedence over astronomy, partly because geometric configurations can exist in the abstract, and partly because "all motion is subsequent to rest, and in nature stasis is always prior. Astronomy gives the theory of moving, and geometry of stationary, bodies; and the motion of the stars is also celebrated in harmonic modulations" (*Inst. arithm*. I. 2, p. 11f).[14] The entire system thus falls into place.

On the level of the individual soul, since the arts provide a systematic

means of rising from accidental to essential, they point to the One, the
Good, and the mind of God. To be trained in them should consequently
have the effect of bringing the human mind into relation with the Good.
Following Plato and Pythagoras, Boethius cites music in particular as
linking the moral with the theoretical. The arguments are familiar
enough not to need special amplification here.[15] However, an example is
taken from arithmetic, where learning an aspect of number does not
simply teach one to act ethically, but by its very nature presents a
moral. The example given is perfect numbers. These are numbers
whose parts add up to themselves. For instance, 6 has a half which is 3,
a third which is 2, and a unit. These all add up to 6. Perfect numbers are
contrasted with superabundant numbers on the one hand, and defective numbers on the other. An example of a superabundant number is
12, whose parts add up to 16; and an example of a defective number is 8,
whose parts add up to 7. Boethius refers to the superabundant
numbers as monsters, like giants or three-headed creatures, who have
more than they should, while the defective numbers, like the one-eyed
Cyclops, have less. Perfect numbers observe an ideal balance harmony
and proportion, and this is the moral: "There is a close parallel in these
things with virtues and vices. For it is rare to find perfect numbers, and
they can easily be enumerated, inasmuch as there are few of them and
they are begotten of an exceedingly constant order. On the other hand,
you will perceive superabundant and defective numbers a long way off,
and there are many of them stretching into infinity. They are not in any
order but are scattered about at random, and they are not generated by
any firm rule" (*Inst. arithm*. I. 20, p. 41f).[16]

As for politics, music is emphasized, for just as there can be harmony
in the soul, so there can be harmony in the body politic. Boethius cites
Plato directly, and, as with the moral side of music, the argument is
probably well enough known not to occupy us here.[17] It is not surprising that an art whose subject is mobile multitudes should relate in some
way to the body politic, since statecraft describes the ideal relations of
numbers of people pursuing their own interests. However, the art of
immobile magnitudes, geometry, also relates to the community in a
very particular way by describing the community's boundaries. This
relation is in a sense self-evident, though it is not often brought to the
fore in discussions of medieval polity. It does not even appear in the
standard edition of the *Ars geometriae*, though I did find such a discussion in a preface to this work contained in Bodleian MS Douce 125,
which to my knowledge has not yet been published.[18] The author first
quotes Varro as saying that in ancient Egypt geometry was necessary to

establish measured territorial boundaries in order to maintain peace among quarrelsome nomads, as well as for measurements which permitted calendrical computations. Second, he says that geometry is useful for mechanics (engineering) and architecture, for medicine (presumably to describe basic principles of anatomic structure), and for philosophy, since it offers a theoretical picture of the workings of the universe. Third, geometry is related to rhetoric since it offers a grounding in reasoned argument.

The third application follows from the study of the various geometric propositions, which teach the principles of deductive argument and are clearly useful for the art of oratory and persuasion. This aspect of geometry suggests a system in which reasoned debate is important, and the references to land measurement, time keeping, architecture, medicine, and astronomy suggest practical public activities based on a rational and objective order. We are looking at an understanding of politics based not just on power but primarily on reason, and presumably exercised not first on the battlefield but in the classroom.

While geometric ideas underpin the orderly community, many of the theoretical principles are still to be found in the science of numerical relations. For example, we have already seen where the numerical contraries are said to be drawn together towards unity by a kind of "friendship and kindred" (*Inst. arithm.* II. 32, p. 125). In the following chapter Boethius describes the parts of the number as being generated through friendship (*Inst. arithm.* II. 33, p. 126: cf. the statement: "Equals are said to stand with each other in the same way as friends and neighbours do," *Inst. arithm.* I. 21, p. 45).[19] Thus arithmetic as well as music represents a harmonious community. We should take this reference to friendship and kindred as more than just rhetorical ornament. It is something which not only illustrates the mathematical relation Boethius is attempting to explain but also provides the rudiments of a theory of actual friendship. For example, friends may pursue various, even contrary, interests, but are nevertheless drawn by a common bond and stand in equality to each other. The extension of friends into kindred and neighbours suggests that beyond private relationships these terms describe the interaction of fellow-citizens.

As with geometry, there is a sense in which these concepts are designed to lead one from the random and irrational to a systematic idea of relationship based on essential truth. We can see something of this in Boethius's discussion of the mean (*medietas*). The notion of the mean is Aristotelean, and Boethius also adopts the idea that the mean is a harmonic proportion.[20] There are three fundamental kinds of mean, the arithmetic, the geometric and the musical or harmonic. To these are added antigeometric and antiharmonic means to make up ten, the number of the Ten Predicates (which relates to dialectic: see *Inst. arithm.* II. 41, p. 139). We do not need to go any further into the "anti" means, but the primary ones provide the basis for a political reference.

The arithmetic mean is the simplest of the three (it must not be confused with the arithmetic mean of modern statistics). It describes a number an equal distance from two extremes. For example, the arithmetic mean between 10 and 40 is 25, a number which is separated from each extreme by 15. It is found by adding the two extremes and halving the sum. For working convenience, this mean can be expressed in modern algebra as: $A = (a+b)/2$. The geometric mean is a term which is proportionally distant from the major and minor extremes. For example, the geometric mean between 10 and 40 is 20, which is twice the minor term and half the major, the proportion being 2:2. It is found by calculating the square root of the product of the extremes, algebraically: $G = \sqrt{ab}$. The harmonic mean is the most complicated of all. It is easiest to understand when the major term is four times the minor, in which case the mean will always be an integer and can be seen in a continuous ratio of 5:8:20. Boethius does the calculation by a sequence of addition, subtraction, multiplication and division, so that it might simply be best to give the formula in its modern algebraic form: $H = 2(ab)/(a+b)$.[21] Thus the harmonic mean between 10 and 40 is 16. One notices that the arithmetic mean is closest of the three to the major term, the geometric mean is middle, and the harmonic mean is nearest the minor term. The relationship among the means between 10 and 40 is that each higher mean is 1.25 times the next lower, or 0.8 times the one above. Thus the geometric mean is itself the geometric mean between the harmonic and the arithmetic, and this relationship is constant when the proportion between major and minor terms is 4:1. (Further, if within this proportion the minor term is a multiple of 10, all three means will be integers.)

All this has a direct bearing on images of statecraft.[22] For it allows Boethius to associate the three arts of arithmetic, music, and geometry with the three kinds of government – monarchy, aristocracy, and democracy – discussed especially in Cicero's *De re publica*: "Arithmetic can be compared to a state which is governed by the few, since the greater proportion rests in its minor terms. The harmonic mean is a state governed by its nobles, since the greater proportion is found in its major terms. The geometric mean represents a popular or democratic state, since it is made up proportionally of major and minor terms equally" (*Inst. arithm.* II. 45, p. 149).[23] What this signifies is that in arithmetic the proportion of the scale below the mean is greater than that above (taking the minor term as a proportion of the mean, and comparing it with the mean as a proportion of the major term). In music the proportion of the scale above the mean is greater than that below (using the same method). In geometry the two are equal, so there is a kind of proportional balance between mean and extremes. Further, since the geometric mean is itself a mean between the other two, it represents a harmonizing of all three, possibly giving us a mathematical basis for Cicero's statement that the best system of government is a mixture of the three.[24]

A final instance of political imagery lies in Boethius's use of the term *duces* or dukes (lit. "leaders") to describe major terms in certain relationships, and *comites* or counts (lit. "companions") to describe minor ones (see e.g. *Inst. arithm.* I. 24, p. 49f). The *duces* and *comites* describe fractional relationships with integers that are analogous with the relationships among means and extremes (it is not stated, but might well be understood, that the integer or mean is the "prince" which stands amidst that part of the system).

So far we have not discussed the trivium, and in one sense it should not be necessary to make a special argument for its relationship with the art of politics. Cicero mentions that it is the power of reason which allows humans to distinguish words and thus to communicate. Speech is a prerequisite for community, and grammar is a prerequisite for speech, so the importance of grammar for social structure is clear.[25] Rhetoric has a twofold purpose, first to describe a kind of virtue in the orator, and second to inform the work of deliberative and judicial bodies (this too is Ciceronian, but is influential in medieval rhetoric).[26] As for dialectic, at one level it is simply too abstruse for practical affairs; but at a more elementary level it concerns itself with reasoning, and with distinguishing truth from falsehood. In a sense it is the art of first principles, and it concerns itself with definitions and with methods of discerning reality.

Like the quadrivium the trivium concerns itself with means, but these means are the virtues of human conduct, both private and public. There is a governmental image in this sense of virtue, which springs from Aristotle and is echoed by Cicero, but which is found in such writers as Alcuin of York: "Virtue embraces all parts of the soul, governing and ruling the entire soul by its sovereignty, and works to tame wrath and banish excessive desire" (*Disputatio de rhetorica et de virtutibus*, PL 101:960).[27] Through virtue the person becomes a kind of monarchy where the rational soul is the mean between the extremes of repulsion and attraction signified by the irascible and appetitive souls. Using phraseology taken from Numbers 20:17, etc., but referring, too, to the precepts of philosophers, Alcuin says, "Let us take the King's Highway, turning neither to the right nor to the left" (*Disputatio, PL* 101:960),[28] and this terminology informs a great deal of medieval thinking about ideal conduct.

We can now begin to draw some conclusions. On the practical level the arts provide a rational and ethical underpinning for such things as trade, boundaries, and the calendar. However, another theme also runs through the material. For each of the subjects in the quadrivium is in itself a model kingdom or polity. Arithmetic, geometry, music, and astronomy each presents us with the possibility of some kind of extreme which is nonetheless tempered and brought into order by the mean or virtue of its art.[29] The diversity of number admits nothing but chaos unless it can be arranged by unity which not only participates in the entire system but also provides the centre about which the entire system is displayed. However, important as unity is, it is nevertheless not the arithmetic mean, so it is itself balanced with the other numbers rather than being the balance. In geometry, lines and shapes could have no pattern unless they moved from point to point. In a theoretical sense the point supplies the centre which holds the entire system together. In neither art, though, does the centre simply swallow up the periphery. While periphery without centre would result in anarchy, centre without periphery would result in a kind of tyranny. Indeed, since the periphery is generated from the centre, without the periphery the centre would have no visible expression: it would remain a potential rather than an actual force, completely withdrawn and completely unknown.

In music the outer extreme is cacophony, absolute noise. In any mode the centre can be defined as the Final, while the Octave, Fourth and Fifth serve further to define the mode. Music gives the model of a system in which a number of parts are arranged so that they can move freely but not collide. Again, the Final of the mode is by no means the entire melody, but only one aspect of it: as in arithmetic it is the mean or virtue of the art which allows various notes (which by nature are contraries and ought to cancel each other out) to be balanced and reconciled. Astronomy demonstrates with solid bodies what music does with abstract forms. It is the mean which allows the entire system to orbit in harmony – to be in fact a system – and this harmony provides the best possible way in which all objects may move and yet avoid collision.

In the trivium the imagery is perhaps not as striking as it is in the quadrivium, but there is still something to be said. All of these are arts of the word. Grammar shows the logical parts of discourse, and how disparate words all work together to form meaningful statements within a meaningful language (in a sense its mean is meaning itself). Rhetoric shows the extremes of praise and blame (which are related to attraction and repulsion, and thus to the appetitive and irascible souls) balanced by argument. This argument aims not merely at agreement as to the solution of a problem, but also at the policy or course of action which should flow from that agreement. And so its mean, or virtue, is right conduct. When the orator is virtuous, then that itself personifies the mean. Dialectic attempts to find order and classification where at first there seems only to be random distribution. However, it also presents the mean between assertion and denial, and attempts to use both in order to develop knowledge.

The grand model demonstrated by the arts informs both universal and personal levels. On the one hand the cosmos is a polity embracing all orders of being, governed by God who is its Creator. On the other hand the self is a tiny kingdom where the monarch Reason ought to govern both body and passions. Here as in the arts the end is neither to allow the passions to run helter-skelter with the entire being nor to allow reason to suppress all but itself. Ideally the self is a free-associating commonwealth in which all parts should find their own mean, and all means should fit together harmoniously. It is the intelligence (the highest faculty of the soul) which is the mean or virtue of the self, and which allows the unified reason and the diverse passions to live in community.

From this it should be evident that a theory of governance can be inferred. If the "King's Highway" is the road of virtue, and if the reason governs the passions royally, then one can turn the analogy around to see an actual king as properly embodying both virtue and reason. The ideal commonwealth is like an arithmetical system in which the one king rules and orders the many subjects. It is like a geometric system in which the shape of the nation begins and ends in a single point. It is like a musical system in which all levels of the society come together in harmony, and it is like a celestial system in which all the various classes and interests within the community follow their own paths, but do not collide, and together constitute one organism. Likewise, the ideal commonwealth is marked by the precision of its language, its ability to agree on and set in motion good policy, and its ability to discern truth from falsehood.

Just as the democratic mean, the geometric, is itself the mean between the arithmetic and the harmonic, so the ideal commonwealth allows for a balanced participation of king, nobles, and people. Just as in the other arts the resolution of the tension between centre and periphery is not to eradicate one or the other but rather to set them in balance, so the ideal commonwealth is neither too strictly controlled by its king nor at the mercy of its people. In practical terms this would involve a reciprocal relationship between local and national concerns, private interest and the common good, in which each was free to move in the best possible way so as to avoid collision. Just as in arithmetic unity is not the mean, but is set in balance by the mean, so the king is not the fulcrum of the nation. We might say that it is the law itself which is the mean, the middle term which brings together all the contrary interests in the nation and the virtue which describes the nation's good conduct. In this model the king is not the whole system. Nor is he even the end and purpose of the system. Rather, he is himself part of the system and must also observe the law. Nevertheless he should in some way exemplify the law, and the virtue and justice it seeks to bring about.

In the Christian understanding of such things we see a process of redemption of the natural order. The arts were invented to provide a remedy against the Fall, and the commonwealth was invented to aid in the moral and spiritual improvement of humanity, since ideal law in all its forms encourages and protects good while restraining evil. Christian thinkers took over the arts and identified wisdom (and its law) with Christ. In the Christian nation Christ is the model king, and the human king governs as his vicar. The conflict between Augustine's two cities begins to be resolved, and human government becomes a means of grace.[30]

NOTES

1 The area I know best is the later Anglo-Saxon state, and this paper may be taken as a background study for an understanding of political theory that was drawn from liberal arts studies in the Court School of Alfred the Great, is part of the Benedictine system of education which flourished from the mid-tenth century, and informs Wulfstan's *Institutes of Polity*. This paper is not the place to prove that link, but I am engaged in a larger study of the subject. However, the idea that later Anglo-Saxon government was literate has been accepted. Simon Keynes's argument that by the late tenth century there was a royal secretariat in England has re-

ceived general agreement. See S.D. Keynes, *The Diplomas of King Aethelred 'the Unready' 978–1016* (Cambridge: Cambridge University Press 1980). See also H.R. Loyn, *The Governance of Anglo-Saxon England 500–1087* (London: Edward Arnold 1984), esp. 106–18. The last part of Asser's life of Alfred indicates that the king intended education to improve the entire administration of justice.

2 A contemporary letter asserts, "In your hands Greek teachings have become Roman doctrine," noting Boethius's translations of Pythagoras on music, Ptolemy on astronomy, Nichomachus on arithmetic, Euclid on geometry, Plato on theology, Aristotle on logic, and Archimedes on physics. This letter is cited by Jonathan Barnes, "Boethius and the Study of Logic," found in Margaret Gibson, ed., *Boethius: His Life, Thought and Times* (Oxford: Basil Blackwell 1981), 73. Two recent histories of early medieval philosophy are by John Marenbon: *From the Circle of Alcuin to the School of Auxerre: Logic, Theology and Philosophy in the Early Middle Ages* (Cambridge: Cambridge University Press 1981), and *Early Medieval Philosophy (480–1150): An Introduction* (London: Routledge & Kegan Paul 1983).

3 In addition to the work edited by Margaret Gibson (n. 2), the following will be useful: Henry Chadwick, *Boethius: The Consolations of Music, Logic, Theology and Philosophy* (Oxford: Clarendon Press 1981) and Michael Masi, *Boethius and the Liberal Arts: A Collection of Essays*, Utah Studies in Literature and Linguistics, 18 (Bern: Peter Lang 1982).

4 *Bedae musica quadrata seu mensurata* (Migne, *Patrologia Latina*, vol. 90, col. 919). The Christianizing of Classical philosophy begins with the linking of Classical statements that reason is coeval with God to such scriptural texts as Ecclesiasticus 1:1, and especially with John 1:1, as well as with the linking of Christ to the Wisdom Books through such authorities as I Corinthians 1: 23f. The equating of Reason, Wisdom, and Christ allows a way of integrating the seven liberal arts through the reference in Proverbs 9:1 to the seven pillars of the House of Wisdom (in Christian exegesis the Church). The political aspect of the rule of Christ is made explicit in Prudentius's *Contra Symmachum* II:756–59, where the Roman emperor is described as a junior partner of Christ, as if Christ were in fact the Dean of the Imperial College.

5 All references to the *De institutione arithmetica*, the *De institutione musica* and the *Ars geometriae* (except the MS Douce 125 passages) will be drawn from the edition of Gottfried Friedlein (Leipzig: Teubner 1867), and will be cited in the text in my English translation, with the original Latin given in notes. I am aware of the following translations but have preferred to use my own *Boethius: The Principles of Music*, Calvin M.Bower, trans. (Diss. George Peabody College for Teachers 1966, Ann Arbor: UMI 1967), *Boethi-*

an Number Theory: A Translation of the "De Institutione Arithmetica," Michael
Masi, trans. (Amsterdam: Rodopi 1983). Boethius's reference in *Inst.*
arithm. to the exemplar in the mind of God is echoed in *De cons. phil.* III.
metrum ix, which shows the Platonic origin of this idea.

6 Hinc enim quattuor elementorum multitudo mutuata est, hinc temporum
  vices, hinc motus astrorum caelique conversio.

7 Omnia, quae ex contrariis consisterent, armonia quadam coniungi atque
  componi. Est enim armonia plurimorum adunatio et dissidentium con-
  sensio. The idea is derived from Aristotle's *De anima* i. 4, 407b.

8 ... nullis propriis principiis nixum, sed natura semper errans a boni defini-
  tione principii.

9 Nam nimiam cupiditatem iraeque immodicam effrenationem quasi quidem rector animus pura intelligentia roboratus adstringit, et has quodammodo inaequalitatis formas temperata bonitate constituit. This same description appears in Plato's *Republic* iv. 443, where the function of the
  rational soul is described as holding the irascible and appetitive souls in
  balance. The schema describes the four cardinal virtues. When wisdom,
  courage, and temperance are in harmony, then justice results. The same
  schema describes the state, the three aspects of the soul being characterized by the guardians, the soldiers, and the artisans.

10 Hoc igitur illud quadruvium est, quo his viandum sit, quibus excellentior
   animus a nobiscum procreatis sensibus ad intelligentiae certiora perducitur.

11 This idea comes from Nichomachus of Gerasa (second century A.D.). See
   John Caldwell, "The *De institutione arithmetica* and the *De institutione*
   musica," in Gibson, ed., *Boethius*, 136f. See also in the same volume Alison
   White, "Boethius in the Medieval Quadrivium," 162–205.

12 Primum autem numerum id est binarium, unitas enim, ut in arithmeticis
   est dictum, numerus non est, sed fons et origo numerorum.

13 Quae scilicet, cum sint contraria, in unam tamen quodammodo amicitiam
   cognationemque miscentur et illius unitatis informatione atque regimento
   unum numeri corpus efficiunt.

14 Omnis motus est post quietem et natura semper statio prior est, mobili-
   um vero astronomia, immobilium geometria doctrina est; vel quod armo-
   nicis modulationibus motus ipse celebratur astrorum.

15 Discussion of these ideas can be found in the *Republic*, Book vii, and in
   Boethius, *Inst. mus.* I. 1.

16 Est autem in his quoque magna similitudo virtutis et vitii. Perfectos enim
   numeros rarenter invenies, eosque facile numerabiles, quippe qui pauci
   sint et nimis constanti ordine procreati. At vero superfluos ac deminutos
   longe multos infinitosque repperies, nec ullis ordinibus passim inordina-
   teque dispositos et a nullo certo fine generatos.

17 See *Republic* iii, and *Inst. mus.* I. 1.

18 The *Summary Catalogue* assigns this MS to the second half of the tenth century. It is a very elegant book and appears to be written in an Insular hand. The superscript is: *IN NOMINE TRINO DIVINO/ INCIPIUNT LIBRI ANNICII MANLII SEVERINI BOETII ARTIS GEOMETRICAE ET ARITHME-TRICAE NUMERO QUINQUE AB EOCLIDE TRANSLATI DE GRECO IN LATINUM,* and the sub-caption is *REGULA ARTIS SEVMETRIAE QUAE EST FONS SENSUUM ET ORIGO DICTIONUM.* I am grateful to the Keeper of Manuscripts and to the staff of the Bodleian Library, Oxford, for patient, kind, and able assistance.

19 Quemadmodum amicus amico amicus est, vicinusque vicino [vicinus], ita dicitur aequalis aequali [aequalis].

20 The concept of the mean is essential to Aristotelian thought. A virtue is the mean between defect and excess (*N. eth.* ii. 6 1106b). Distributive justice involves a geometric mean, while corrective justice involves an arithmetic one (*N. eth.* v. 4 1132a); and money is determined by demand as the mean or middle term of reciprocal justice (*N. eth.* v. 5 1132b). The mean of politics is the common interest (*Pol.* iii. 12 1282b). The mean is the middle term of a syllogism, while in poetry it is metaphor (*Poetics* 22 1459a). To know the middle term is to know the cause or reason of the thing: "Quick wit is a faculty of hitting upon the middle term instantaneously" (*Post. an.* i. 34 89b).

21 Working from the text, let a be the minor term and b the major: (1) add a and b; (2) subtract a from b; (3) multiply the result of 2 by a; (4) divide the result of 3 by the result of 1; (5) add a to the result of 4. This readily works out as $H = [(a[b-a])/(a+b)]+a$, which reduces to $H = 2(ab)/(a+b)$.

22 Plato too uses mathematical formulae to describe political relations, as when Socrates is made to argue that the cycle of a divine race is contained in a perfect number while the cycle of a human race is expressed by a geometric number (*Republic* viii. 546), and that tyrannical, oligarchic and kingly pleasure can be compared geometrically (*Republic* ix. 587).

23 Atque ideo arithmetica quidem rei publicae comparatur, quae paucis regitur, id circo quod in minoribus eius terminis maior proportio sit. Musicam vero medietatem optimatium dicunt esse rempublicam ideo, quod in maioribus terminis maior proportionalitas invenitur. Geometrica medietas popularis quodammodo ex exaequatae civitatis est. Namque vel in maioribus vel in minoribus aequali omnium proportionalitate componitur.

24 *De re publica* I. xxix.

25 Cicero's comment is taken from *De re publica* II. xxi. See also Aristotle, *Pol.* I. 2 1253a.

26 See George A. Kennedy, *Classical Rhetoric and its Christian and Secular Tradi-*

tion From Ancient to Modern Times (London: Croom Helm 1980), esp. on Alcuin, 182ff.

27 Virtus vero omnes animae partes amplectitur, omnemque animam suo imperio gubernat et regit: ut et iracundiam domet et cupiditates amoveat. Compare Aristotle, *Politics*, i. 5 4254b; Cicero, *De re publica* iii. xxv. 37, and Augustine, *De civitate Dei* xix. 21.

28 Via regia nobis gradiendum, neque ad dexteram, neque ad sinistram declinandum. This Scriptural reference is given to illustrate the philosophical notion that virtues are means. Compare Abbo of Fleury's description of King Edmund of East Anglia: "gradiensque uia regia nec declinabat ad dexteram, extollendo se de meritis, nec ad sinistram, succumbendo uitiis humanae fragilitatis," Michael Winterbottom, ed., *Three Lives of English Saints* (Toronto: Pontifical Institute of Mediaeval Studies 1972), 71. There is a double sense here both that the middle road is the straight and narrow way of God, and that it is the appropriate way for a king, who in ideal terms is someone who has learned to govern himself before he governs others.

29 Cf. Aristotle, *N. eth.* ii. 6 1106b.

30 The basic concept of this paper was hatched while Archie Malloch and I were both on the Senate of McGill University and were both concerned with issues of university governance. Some of the ideas (such as the notion that the arts provide models of polity) were worked out in discussion with him. I am deeply grateful for a friendship of seventeen years, and for the precept and example he has given in the hard service of academic justice.

James Joyce – Literary Engineer

Mechanization Takes Command, the title of art historian Siegfried Giedion's anonymous history of cultural objects, has provided one of the key descriptive tags of our century. The "machine" not only became universal in its domination of the world's everyday activity, it also became a major preoccupation of artists. Whether adulatory like Futurist paeans of praise, or satiric like Dadaism, or reflective like Cubism and Constructivism, mechanization invaded the visual arts. It also invaded the arts of literature and music, architecture, and the dance, leading ultimately to our uneasy contemporary alliances between art and technology.

It is in this context that during the composition of *Finnegans Wake*, James Joyce described himself to Harriet Shaw Weaver as one of the greatest engineers, if not the greatest, in addition to being a great musician, a great philosopher, and a host of other things. While the remark may ring of Celtic bravado, its announcement was accompanied by a stricture concerning Joyce's seriousness about what he was doing and by a description of how he was in the process of designing a wheel and squaring the circle.

Comparing the artist and the engineer was a familiar theme for Joyce and his contemporaries. Having grown up during a thirty-year period which Péguy described as having seen more change than the previous 3000 years, their sensibilities were acutely tuned to tools, mechanisms, and human invention. Paul Valéry, participating in the process of reviving and reevaluating Leonardo's image, argued that the method of the engineer and that of the poet were the same. He re-articulates a frequent Renaissance theme exemplified by George Puttenham's statement in his 1589 *Arte of English Poesie*: "Wherefore such persons as be illuminated with the brightest irradiations of knowledge and of the veritie and due proportion of things, they are called by the learned men ... *euphantasiote*, and of this sorte of phantasie are all good Poets, notable Captaines stratagematique, all cunning artificers and enginers, all Legislators Polititiens & Counsellours of estate, in whose exercises the inventive part is most employed and is to the sound & true judgement of man most needful."[1] Views such as these, articulated by many Renaissance writers on poetry, would also have been endorsed by Vico, who in *Finnegans Wake* was one of Joyce's prime guides concerning poetic knowledge.

Let us reflect for a moment on the particular historical context in which Joyce matured as an artist. Within the five years before Joyce was born, Edison developed both sound recording and the electric light. During the early years of Joyce's life the Eiffel tower was erected; Lumière explored moving pictures; Marie Curie discovered radium; Marconi completed the first transatlantic broadcast; the Wright brothers developed the airplane; Einstein articulated the Theory of Relativity; and Ford, through the introduction of the assembly line into the production of motor cars, completed the process by which mass mechanization took command.

All of these creations and most of their creators appear in various parts of *Finnegans Wake*. In fact, viewed retrospectively, Joyce appears preoccupied with the images of constructors, builders, and other cunning artificers. Not only does Daedalus appear in *A Portrait of the Artist* (as the figure of classical mythology reflected in Stephen Dedalus's name), but he is placed in juxtaposition with that other cunning artificer god, Hephaestos or Vulcan (figuratively reflected in the handicapped Dean of Studies) in the scene in which Stephen debates with the Dean, who is engaged in lighting the fire in the Physics Theatre. Bloom's persona is paralleled with the cunning Ulysses, who was a constructor as well as navigator. The "everyman," who is the dreamer of the *Wake*, is related through the dream to a variety of artificers beginning with the hod carrier, an ironic image of the "masterbuilder," Tim Finnegan, and including a multitude of various architects, builders, poets and other creators.[2] The Latin root of engineer, *ingenium*, implying cunning, plays behind the surface everyday meaning in all of these renditions of artificers.

In spite of our usual preoccupation with the mythic dimensions of Joyce's last two major works, technology also dominates their content, their construction, and their spirit. Part of the opening of *Finnegans Wake* presents images of towers, including not only the Eiffel Tower, but the

Woolworth Building and other skyscrapers. The climax of the *Wake* involves a technical debate between Patrick and the Archdruid about the nature of light and colour ("Rhythm and Color at Park Mooting"), as well as a remarkable discussion of code and fragmentation. The climax of *Ulysses* in the Circe section takes place in what, viewed today from the perspective of Genet's *Le Balcon*, can be described as Bella Cohen's fantasy machine, reminding us of the mechanics of the Freudian dream work; while the resolution of the book occurs in what Joyce himself described as the mathematical catechism of the Ithaca section where Bloom returns home with Stephen and reviews the events of the day. In both works Joyce has developed Mallarmé's sense of the book as a literary machine; the theme of self-consciousness concerning a book about a book and books themselves dominates the dream of the *Wake*. As Marshall McLuhan argued in "Joyce, Mallarmé and the Press,"[3] Mallarmé interpreted the marriage between book and machine in terms of the revolution occurring in popular culture. In his correspondence Malcolm Lowry provides a remarkable explanation of this newly emerging sense of the modern work of art as a machine:

It can be regarded as a kind of symphony, or in another way a kind of opera – or even a horse opera. It is hot music, a poem, a song, a tragedy, a comedy, a farce and so forth. It is superficial, profound, entertaining and boring, according to taste. It is a prophecy, a political warning, a cryptogram, a preposterous movie, and a writing on the wall. It can even be regarded as a sort of machine: it works too, believe me, as I have found out.[4].

Lowry's letter describing his own writing can just as easily describe Joyce's or for that matter, Proust's, for everything Lowry says applies at the very least equally as well to *Ulysses* and *Finnegans Wake*. This is hardly surprising when we remind ourselves that Joyce was the contemporary of Duchamp, Léger, the Dadaists, and the Futurists.

The technological world as image-symbol attracted Joyce's creative interest, for it provided a means of inter-relating various aspects of the world in which he lived: his political interests (a "restrained" socialist-anarchism); his social milieu where the image of urbanization and inter-nationalization fascinated him; his vision of a new Renaissance which ought to produce a modern Leonardo (although Joyce seldom speaks of Leonardo, he once compared his method of note taking and construction to that of Leonardo); his interest in the critique of psychoanalysis, that is Freud's dream-work and the libidinal machines which treat fantasy and desire as the work of mental engineering; and finally, the process of mechanization which appealed to the way that he found problems of technique to be central to creative work. His reinterpretation of the Aristotelian sense of art as *techne* in the context of his vision of the contemporary world utilized technical images, such as the famous passage on art as vivisection in *Stephen Hero*. The groundplan of *Ulysses*, first printed in Stuart Gilbert's *James Joyce's Ulysses* and since presented in expanded form in Ellmann,[5] reflects the multiplicity of modes coexistent within this book. *Ulysses* functions just as Lowry's account says modern works of art function. It demonstrates a new sense of construction, a new way of realizing a vision of a pluralist anarchy within an ordered "chaosmos" (*FW* 118.21). The action and structure of *Ulysses* reflect the real mechanical fragmentation of everyday life in modern cities. The city as a form is an appropriate interest for an artist-engineer, just as the anatomy of the body is; both interests, in fact, are reflected in the notebooks of Leonardo da Vinci.

The action of *Ulysses* occurs in a cityscape within which a pseudo-artisan, pseudo-hero, the ad salesman Leopold Bloom, wanders throughout one day in June. Bloom's wanderings through time and space are related to the organs of the body and to specific sign-symbols paralleling specific episodes of the Odyssey whose epic mode is itself fragmented by a multiplicity of stylistic devices. Thus Dublin emerges as a complex technological concept. The formation and shaping of *Ulysses* (which mirrors Dublin) is marked by intricate interweaving of technology and society, the most obvious example being the use of the trams, printing presses, and the devices of rhetoric in the Aeolus section which resonates with Mallarmé's poetic treatment of the newspaper as a new landscape.[6] In the Oxen of the Sun section at the lying-in hospital, the same technical process manifests itself in the figure through which a comic history of the development of English literature reflects a history of the development of the embryo and the birth process. In the conclusion, the counterpointing of the intense desiring machine generated by Molly's libido in her soliloquy in Penelope,[7] the closing section and the almost science fiction-like mathematical catechism of Ithaca, would appear the only possible resolution.

This fascination with technology and the art of the engineer should not lead us to thinking of Joyce as a technological enthusiast (such as some of the Futurists or early Cubists). Neither should it suggest that like his *alter-ego*, enemy figure, Wyndham Lewis, who severely criticized *Ulysses'* preoccupation with the time sense of the new industrial world, Joyce became an enemy of the mechanical world and developed a retrogressive fascism. The connection between Joyce's awareness of technology and his concern for time is well set forth by his friend Frank Budgen in speaking of the making of *Ulysses*:

All the characters in *Ulysses* have just that social time sense that is part of the general social mentality of the period, and no more. This arises out of the necessity for coordinating their daily social movements. It is purely a technical thing, born of mechanical development. James Watt invented the steam engine, and the steam engine begat the locomotive, and the locomotive begat the time-table, forcing people to grapple with its complexities and think in minutes where their great-grandfathers had thought in hours. All their yesterdays, that in an earlier age would have been quietly buried in the hope of a glorious resurrection as myth, lie embalmed in the files of newspapers and snapshot albums. They have suffered the influence of the penny post, telegraph and telephone – all social institutions working to a close time-table. But the principal element in forming that social time sense is the means of locomotion. The discoveries of the astronomer and the mathematician have less immediate effect on this sense than the electrification of the suburban lines. Light and the heavenly bodies are doing what they always did, but the wheels of mechanical civilization are ever accelerating.[8]

Stephen, whose obsession with time is part of his isolation from society, is the only character who stands outside this perspective. The very rhythmic variations of different moments of the day which become part of Bloom's movement as well as of the rhythm of *Ulysses* reflect the all-pervasive nature of social time as mediated through the technical, social and natural machines[9] within which man is entangled – some of the nets from which the youthful Stephen thought escape was possible. For Bloom, though, it is clear that the social machine is part of the shaping of his psyche, for even his escape from the citizen in the Cyclops section, which is realized through a Utopian belief in social engineering that permits the vision of a new Bloomoosalem by Elijah Ben Bloom, is rooted in the new world of mechanization and technology. Not only does the mechanical, the technological and their influence on the temporal dominate the daily consciousness of the characters, it also provides the basis for the comic-satiric mode of shaping a contemporary comic epic poem through the construction of a set of chapters which are uniquely styled miniature epics (or *epyllia*, a form whose relevance to contemporary literature has previously been stressed by Marshall McLuhan). Like Chaplin, Joyce was aware that the comic vision of the contemporary world in which Bloom exists could only be realized through an awareness of the inter-relation between the technological world of mechanization and those social and psychological machines that Gilles Deleuze has so thoroughly described in his various works.

This concern with the technical surface and the machine-like provided Joyce with a natural route to humour, since the machine creates natural discontinuities in the flow of life. The stuttering of HCE, who sees himself in the dream of the *Wake* as a series of machines, breaks up the life flow of ALP and criticizes the myth of Freud's Oedipal family. Joyce's "comedy" of letters, *Finnegans Wake*, plays over the surfaces of everyday life, just as Bloom's peregrinations through the city of Dublin had done in *Ulysses*. The discrete temporal moments of such dislocation create a humour of surfaces which avoids the sublime or the profound, the heights or the depths, except in rare moments where a surface suggests depth as in Stephen's and Molly's genuine soliloquies.

A sense of the surface of things as providing comic perspective would be for many of us characteristically Celtic, associated with John Joyce's tale-telling. This Celtic sense of humour attracted Joyce to Lewis Carroll as well as to the great tradition of neoclassical satirists – Ben Jonson, Pope, Sterne, and especially the Irish Dean, Jonathan Swift.[10] It is said of "Feenichts Playhouse," (the children's microdrama within the drama of *Finnegans Wake*), "your wildeshaweshowe moves swiftly sterneward!" (*FW*, 256.13). The satiric thrust of the *Wake* is described in the mechanical terms of a ship moving through the sea – "a stern poise for a swift pounce" (*FW* 282.7). The essence of Joyce's comic technique is contained in his analysis of Popean heroic couplets; but that analysis takes place during a mathematics lesson involving signs of the technological world: "A Tullagrove pole to the Height of County Fearmanagh has a septain inclinaison and the graphplot for all the functions in Lower County Monachan, whereat samething is rivisible by nighttim, may be involted into the zeroic couplet, palls pell inhis heventh glike noughty times, ∞ find, if you are not literally coefficient, how minney combinaisies and permutandies can be played on the international surd!" (*FW*, 284:5–14).

Joyce's technique of comic humour has a mathematical precision not unlike that of Lewis Carroll – a concern foreshadowed in the way comedy, humour, and a pseudo-mathematical precision coalesce in the mathematical catechism of the Ithaca section of *Ulysses*. In his Alice books and nonsense writing Carroll discovered the key to a wit of the surfaces in which words "can become like a shunting point and we go from one to the other by a multitude of routes; from which the idea of a book emerges that does not simply tell a history, but an ocean of histories."[11] These portmanteau words and their utilization in a pseudological structure create in Carroll's writings what Deleuze has described as a schizoid-like artistic language, ideally suited to the mechanics of sense and to the comic-anarchic modalities of Joyce. Here is a vision which easily parallels that of the world of Duchamp, Dada, and Cubism, for it embraces both the complexities of sense and the absurd emptiness of the growing technological world.

Joyce's work surely must be viewed from a retrospective point of view providing a perspective comparable to viewing the city of Paris from the Eiffel Tower. In the closing passages of *Finnegans Wake* and the panoramic perspective that the Joyce canon reveals, a Joycean vision emerges formed by an interplay of discontinuities that results from interrelating society, conceived as an organic structure like the human body, with the technical world. In a key passage near the end of the book (FW.614) once again analyzing ALP's famous letter (the book itself), the book is described as a "tetradomational gazebocroticon," a "vicociclometer" consisting of "homely codes" which are fragmented and then reassembled by a "paraidiotic" "clappercoupling" process. This reflects the opening where Here Comes Everybody as man-mountain dreams he is a master builder, Bygmester Finnegan piling "buildung supra buildung" (FW, 4.27) (with puns on the German *Bildung*, education in the sense of paideia) and erecting "in undress maisonry upstanded (joygrantit!), a waalworth of skyerscape of most eyeful hoyth entowerly, erigenating from next to nothing and celescalating the himals and all, hierarchitectitiptitoploftical, with a burning bush abob"(FW, 4.35-5.2).

Throughout, therefore, the *Wake* concerns itself with what Louis Mumford described as human technics. In this opening section the power of the ancient Egyptian and Eastern tower builders is reborn in the modern erectors of skyscrapers and exhibition towers. Once again man manifests his Babel complex, for Joyce's hero participates on the next page in "overgrown babeling!" Just as Barthes has suggested in his essay on the Eiffel Tower, such symbols are supposed to serve one purpose, such as to communicate with God, and yet Babel and such symbols are dreams which "touch much greater depths than that of the theological project."[12] Dada, with its poetic babel deliberately fragmenting communication to sound an alarm, provided Joyce with an insight which links his use of Carrollian language with his continued exploration of technology and technique. Humph, one of the dream manifestations of our hero, HCE, is the Grandada of all rogues whose coming fragments the continuities of traditional tellers of tales. Joyce's comic title of his self-engineered commentary on his own work further underlines this technological and mechanistic intent: *Our Exagmination Round his Factification for Incamination of Work in Progress* with its puns on analyses, fortifications, and facts links the technological stress to the interest in textual interaction which is a prevalent theme of the *Wake*. Factification, combining fortification and fact and fiction, is particularly important for a work that bridged the period between two World Wars and concerns itself with the growth of mechanization and technique, for the *Wake* is also a book concerned with wars.[13]

Battles abound in the *Wake* with the archetype being provided by Napoleon, his militarism and his final battle at Waterloo. Complementing the presence of war and battle, though, is the presence of a contemporary revolution. If the day to which the *Wake* of Holy Saturday leads is Easter Sunday, then its coming can genuinely be announced by an announcement of a " 'Surrection' " – an insurrection as well as a resurrection and probably an erection. Sex, building, revolution, and communion join together in a world where HCE can only produce his own sense of himself "communionistically."[14] Joyce's books are, as Derrida observed, deeply influenced by Hegel, but they are a post-Hegelian vision of a socialist anarchist rather than that of an Hegelian. The *Wake* obviously developed its sense of truth, *in vino veritas*, from the Hegelian definition of truth as a "bacchanalian revel where not a sole is sober," but Joyce turned his *Wake* into a revelation of the comic demonodicy concealed within Hegel's phenomenology. Fundamentally, his conception of the production of a poetic work-in-progress is post-Marxist as well as post-Hegelian and prophetically post-modern.

In both *Ulysses* and the *Wake* media become the bridge between technology and communication, so that as McLuhan was the first to note, Joyce abounds in media references. HCE as hero, like Wyndham Lewis's Bailiff in the *Childermass* or Horace Zagreus in the *Apes of God*, is a broadcaster. But in Joyce's presentation he literally becomes a telecommunications machine, since, like Giedion, Joyce realizes the continuity from mechanical to electrical and electronic devices. In the opening of the barroom scene, the Host, HCE, is "birth of an otion":

their tolvtubular high fidelity daildialler, as modern as tomorrow afternoon and in appearance up to the minute ... equipped with super-shielded umbrella antennas for distance getting and connected by the magnetic links of a Bellini-Tosti coupling system with a vitaltone speaker, capable of capturing skybuddies, harbour craft emittences, key clickings, vaticum cleaners, due to woman formed mobile or man made static and bawling the whowle hamshack and wobble down in an eliminium sounds pound so as to serve him up a melegoturny marygoraumd, eclectrically filtered for allirish earths and ohmes. This harmonic condenser enginium (the Mole) they caused to be worked from a magazine battery ... which was tuned up by twintriodic singulvalvulous pipelines (lackslipping along as if their liffing deepunded on it) with a howdrocephalous enlargement, a gain control of circumcentric megacycles ... (*FW* 309.14–310.7)

The overlayering of the traditional tale-teller with the image of a broadcasting system and hence of a broadcaster indicates a profound social shift – a shift from the ways of transmitting knowledge and information at the level of the neighbourhood or the village to that of the anonymous city composed of ex-villagers. Yet there is another aspect to the image – the humanizing of the technology and the recognition that man himself, even as tale-teller, especially innkeeper-tale-teller is himself a kind of instrument, a kind of machine. At least one displacement occurs in the barroom scene where the running of the Caerholme Event has been presented by TV – an *"admirable verbivocovisual presentment"* (*FW* 341.18–19). Eventually a debate about a battle between Butt and Taff, two puppet-like clown figures, is transmuted into the TV set: *"In the heliotropical noughttime following a fade of transformed Tuff and, pending its viseversion, a metenergic reglow of beaming Batt, the bairdboard bombardment screen, if tastefully taut guranium satin, tends to teleframe and step up to the charge of a light barricade. Down the photoslope in syncopanc ... borne by their carnier walve"* (*FW*, 349.6).

Such scenes clearly demonstrate that the *Wake* presents a continuity between mechanization taking command and the rise of the electric world, since the principle of discontinuity and fragmentation implicit in the former is expanded exponentially in the latter. The design of the language, in fact, parallels the phenomenon of electrification which will eventually through automation produce a super-mechanized technocratic society. The *Wake* recognizes the beginnings of this "taylorised world" in an overlayering of the name of the time-study engineer, Frederick Winslow Taylor, with the late eighteenth-century neo-Platonist, Thomas Taylor. But the media as mediator between other machines and human communication indicate the fundamental social fragmentation and the way that language itself as instrument is a type of machine. The TV in the barroom presents, yet participates in the "abnihilisation of the etym" (*FW*, 353.22), a phrase weaving together war, the destructive transformation of the natural world and the transmutation of language and more particularly of writing in the super-mechanized world.

For Joyce, the text which is a "litter" and an assembly of letters, itself

becomes a machine. The reading of texts – those "curios of signs" –
joins history to psychoanalysis, but the analysts become a group of
technocrats reading the signs projected by the sleeping Yawn – a "map
of the soul's groupography." In the comic perspective of the *Wake*, the
mechanical interrogations of the four old men are themselves exposed
satirically as a technological approach to the dream mechanism. Near
the moment of awakening, language and dreams are both presented in
the language of mechanization, a language suitable to Joyce's "serial
dreams": "Totalled in toldteld and teldtold in tittletell tattle. Why?
Because, graced be Gad and all giddy gadgets, in whose words were the
beginnings, there are two signs to turn to, the yest and the ist, the
wright side and the wronged side..." (*FW*, 597.8). Joyce's serial logic is
dialectic and discontinuous. The dream movement echoes the mechanical movements of the circulatory system in the human body: "Every
talk has his stay ... and all-a-dreams perhapsing under lucksloop at last
are through. Why? It is a sot of a swigswag, systomy dystomy, which
everabody you ever anywhere at all doze" (*FW*, 597.19).

Clive Hart has noted Joyce's use of "serial dreams" which echo the
temporal order of Dunne's "serial universe" based on his conception of
serial time.[15] But it also invokes the whole strategy of the dream, using
the technique of the series, a technique which Joyce shares with Lewis
Carroll as well as with some satirists. Serialism underlies the process of
infinite regression in *Finnegans Wake* by which any portion of the structure appears to be nested in a larger portion, just as one Chinese box is
nested in another. The remark about the "shunting-points," which are
Joyce's words quoted above, is the focal point for such a serialism. In a
very different way, in the Cyclops section of *Ulysses*, the mechanical use
of romance in such presentations as the tale of the hanging is dependent on such serialism. The technique of the series, in fact, is explicitly
borrowed from the serial structure of Lewis Carroll's Alice books where
the production of meaning is achieved through a series of regressions,
such as Humpty Dumpty's endless process of analysis. The strategy
obviously works in a world where individuals can "psoakoonaloose"
(*FW*, 522:34) themselves and Joyce uses it as a strategy for dismantling
"Jungfraud's Messongebook" (*FW*, 460.20), since the schizophrenic
character of the medium in the Circe section of *Ulysses* or in *Finnegans
Wake* creates a parody of the unconscious which is the target of psychoanalysis.

Joyce sees meaning in terms of production, which again has relations
to the way he is rooted in the world of mechanization which has become a second nature. Such a theme of production first enters at the

very beginning of the *Portrait of the Artist* where the artist as baby is in the earlier stages of developing human senses. In a familiar passage from the inquisition of Yawn we learn: "If there is a future in every past that is present *Quis est qui non novit quinnigan* and *Qui quae quot at Quinnigan's Quake!* Stump! His producers are they not his consumers? Your exagmination round his factification for incamination of a warping process. Declaim!" (*FW*, 496.35-7.3). The making process, the seriality of time, the production of meaning and technology as well as self and society all emerge inter-related in the world of "homely codes." Consequently, Joyce can join an account of the mechanics of meaning (which seems to anticipate our modern cybernetic world) when speaking of his *vicociclometer* with ALP's letter, his book, the dream and its symbolic action – all of which are machines in this Joycean world, just as, in the very same sense, the more ordinary recognizable machines. Even the activities of the unconscious are produced in such a process, so that it, too, has analogies with the mechanized world. Joyce parodies this mechanical function of the unconscious in part of his portrait of Shem, the artist brother who "was in his bardic memory low." He presents Shem describing the father figure, "Mr. Humhum, whom history, climate and entertainment made the first of his sept and always up to debt." Shem's activity as poet is described as:

giving unsolicited testimony on behalf of the absent, as glib as eaveswater to those present (who meanwhile, with increasing lack of interest in his semantics, allowed various subconscious smickers to drivel slowly across their fichers), unconsciously explaining, for inkstands, with a meticulosity bordering on the insane, the various meanings of all the different foreign parts of speech he misused and cuttlefishing every lie unshrinkable about all the other people in the story, leaving out, of course, foreconsciously, the simple worf and plague and poison they had cornered him about until there was not a snoozer among them but was utterly undeceived in the heel of the reel by the recital of the rigmarole.   (*FW*, 173.28-44)

The telling of the dream tale is cinematic (which is mechanized) and speaks the language of the unconscious as the book declares in the familiar "roll away the reel world, the reel world, the reel world" (*FW*, 64.25). Elsewhere, in dealing with the deciphering of letters in the *Wake*, I have shown the close connection between the psychoanalytic themes, the interpretive themes and the mechanics of sense.[16] Relating those themes to the interest of the *Wake* in the world of mechanization takes command and the rise of the electric world with its communication media, clearly shows that Joyce, as McLuhan had realized in his own work, treats the technological world as an extension of the human psyche and senses. If the work Joyce conceives can engage with the world of technology and yet somehow resolve itself "communionistically," it is certainly worth remembering what Marx wrote:

Just as music alone awakens in man the sense of music, and just as the most beautiful music has *no* sense for the unmusical ear ... the *senses* of the social man are *other* senses than those of the nonsocial man. Only through the objectively unfolded richness of man's essential being is the richness of subjective *human* sensibility (a musical ear, an eye for beauty of form – in short, *senses* capable of human gratification, senses affirming themselves as essential powers of *man*) either cultivated or brought into being. For not only the five senses but also the so-called mental senses – the practical senses (will, love, etc.) – in a word, *human sense* – the human nature of the senses – comes to be by virtue of its object, by virtue of *humanized* nature. The *forming* of the five senses is a labor of the entire history of the world down to the present.[17]

From an aesthetic perspective, the *Wake* is involved in exploring the same history of the formation of humanized nature and social man. Joyce is often satiric, as we have seen in his treatment of technology, and black humour dominates the way he presents the record of human battles. Yet he sees the frequency of war as involved in the failure of the labour of forming a sense of man, for "The war is in words and the wood is the world," the *Wake* proclaims (*FW*, 98.34–5). The conclusion of the *Wake* is to be a waking into peace (though ambivalently perhaps the peace of death), yet also the assertion of the life energy of the erotic, the flow of ALP who in her soliloquy at one point says: "The rollcky road adondering. We can sit us down on the heathery benn, me on you, in quolm unconsciounce. To scand the arising. Out from Drumleek. It was there Evora told me I had best. If I ever. When the moon of mourning is set and gone. Over Glinaduna. Lonu nula. Ourselves, oursouls alone. At the site of salvocean. And watch would the letter you're wanting be coming may be. And cast ashore. That I prays for be mains of me draims" (*FW*, 623.24). The structure of puns, though, weaves the substratum of the technological structure of the city as an undertone in "I prays for be mains of me draims" with the obvious play on mains and drains. But Anna as the symbol of Eros, the living energy, the flows of libido and desire, is also related to the very nature of the world of machines and techniques. One remarkable passage about Anna Livia makes this clear: "Here she is, Amnisty Ann! Call her calamity electrifies man. No electress at all but old Moppa Necessity, angin mother of injons" (*FW*, 207.27).

All of the same themes that we have been discussing play a major role in the climactic passages of book IV of the *Wake*, the debate between Patrick and the Archdruid on the nature of light and colour and the description of the book itself. In one of the key concluding passages of the *Wake*, [18] Joyce describes his "tetradomational gazebocroticon" mentioned above: "autokinatonetically preprovided with a clappercoupling smeltingworks exprogressive process ... receives through a portal vein the dialytically separated elements of precedent decomposition for the very petpurpose of subsequent recombination so that the heroticisms, catastrophes and eccentricities transmitted by the ancient legacy of the past, type by tope, letter from litter, word at ward ... may be there for you" (*FW*, 614.31–15.8).

As I mentioned earlier, here there is a clear connection between the book as a machine and the process of expression as a process of production, which integrates the book with the technological world. In fact, Joyce's whole comic-satiric thrust becomes associated with the project of designing a dialectical dialogic language for coping with the logic of sense to comprehend a world of revolutions. For this reason, as we have seen, the opening cry of Book IV is a broadcast announcing the moments of resurrection, insurrection, and revolution linking motifs of Easter, Irish revolution and the coming of a new age where mechanization has not taken command but been humanized by a newly produced human sensorium, itself the product of the progressive process. In such a world Joyce, like Proust, seeks for a mode of transverse communications. As Gilles Deleuze has described it: "in a world reduced to a multiplicity of chaos [i.e., Joyce's "chaosmos" (*FW*, 118.21)], it is only the formal structure of the work of art, insofar as it does not refer to anything else, which can serve as unity – afterwards (or as Umberto Eco says 'the work as a whole proposes new linguistic conventions to which it submits, and itself becomes key to its own code')"[19] i.e., Joyce's "gave me the keys to dreamland" (*FW*, 615.28).

As in Proust, only more systematically and complexly, *Ulysses* and *Finnegans Wake* are unified on a transverse dimension. In other words, the language of Joyce's dream (as the language of his comic epic of Dublin) is constructed so as to provide its own interrelationships. Dublin is not the object of Joyce's writing, but part of a code he employs to create an international perspective on the city, the problems of its ensnarement in its own regionalism and nationalism which make it characteristic of all European cities. The simultaneous critique of mechanization taking command (which Joyce shares with the Dadaists and Surrealists) and the vision of humanizing technology in the interest of creating a new man – a romantic Utopianism that the socialist anarchist Joyce incorporated into his vision (which he shares with the Cubists and Constructivists) – can only be realized in a transverse mode of communication. This provided a way of achieving what Dewey described as communion within a fragmented, antagonistic, divisive world marked in Joyce's lifetime by a series of major wars, wars which disrupted his own life and possibly contributed to his early death.

The *Wake* reminds us of this in its urge to have us "communicake with the original sinse" and to realize this communication and participation through our communionistic participation in the bacchanalian revels of our taletelling innkeeper who dreams he is a masterbuilder building the new nature of social man. In the process Joyce is a producer of a literary machine, which is productive of truth and communication. He is the greatest engineer because his literary machine is a perpetual motion machine, a constantly recursive circle, yet structured dialectically (and thus dialogically) in four-part structures which characterize the entire work at a variety of levels. The individual parts within the work are themselves structured in sets of four and there even is a four-part structure which often establishes the logical base for the structure of the sentences themselves. Therefore, Joyce can see his literary engineering as encompassing his creative and intellectual capabilities and even contributing to his Utopian vision – "Wait till Finnegan Wakes."

NOTES

All references to *Finnegans Wake* are to the Viking edition (New York 1959) and are cited as *FW* with page references given in the text.

1 George Puttenham, *The Arte of English Poesie*. ed., Gladys Doidge Willcock & Alice Walker (Cambridge: The University Press 1936), 19–20. I have not modernized the spelling of Puttenham's sixteenth-century text to call attention that what I believe to be overtones carried by the particular spelling of certain words. Apart from recognizing that orthography provided possibilities for certain rhetorical figures in Renaissance literature, it also seemed in keeping with the Joycean spirit of the essay.

2 The term "everyman" should also suggest the relation of the dreamer to

what French critics discuss (e.g., Jean Baudrillard) as the *quotidienneté*, everyday life. Both Bloom and the dreamer of the *Wake* are important in the way they are participants in the everyday life of modern cities: Dublin and the major cities of Europe which Joyce knew well.

3 Marshall McLuhan, "Joyce, Mallarmé and the Press," in *Interior Landscape: The Literary Criticism of Marshall McLuhan*, ed. Eugene McNamara (Toronto: McGraw-Hill in association with the University of Windsor Press 1969), 5–21.

4 Malcolm Lowry, *Selected Letters*, eds. Harvey Breit and Margerie Bonne (Philadelphia: Lippincott 1965), 66.

5 See Richard Ellmann, *Ulysses on the Liffey* (New York: Oxford University Press 1972), Appendix (between pp. 187 & 189).

6 McLuhan, "Joyce, Mallarmé and the Press," 13–16, 18–19.

7 I have deliberately borrowed the phraseology from Gilles Deleuze: "For desiring-machines are the fundamental category of the economy of desire: they produce a body without organs all by themselves, and make no distinction between the agents and their own parts, or between the relations of production and their own relations, or between social order and technology." Gilles Deleuze and Felix Guattari, *Anti-Oedipus* (New York: Viking Press 1977), 32. See also pp. 36ff, Section 5, "The Machines."

8 Frank Budgen, *James Joyce and the Making of Ulysses* (Bloomington: Indiana University Press 1960), 129.

9 Again "natural machines" suggests Deleuze's concept of machine which includes parts of natural creatures. G. Deleuze and F. Guattari, *Anti-Oedipus*, 36.

10 Donald F. Theall, "Sound, Sense and the Enveloping Facts: Inspecting the Wit's Waste of an Unheavenly Body," *English Studies in Canada* I, no. 1 (Spring 1975): 99.

11 Michel Butor, *Introduction aux fragments de "Finnegans Wake"* (Paris: Gallimard 1962), 12 [trans. my own].

12 Roland Barthes, *The Eiffel Tower and Other Mythologies*, trans. Richard Howard (New York: Hill and Wang 1979), 7.

13 Donald F. Theall, "Sendance of Sundance: Sense, Communication and Community in *Finnegans Wake*," *Canadian Journal of Irish Studies* 6, no. 1 (June 1980): 3.

14 See Donald F. Theall, "Joyce, Eros and 'Array! Surrection!' " in *Myth and Reality in Irish Literature*, ed. Joseph Ronsley (Waterloo, ON.: Wilfrid Laurier University Press 1977), 239–54.

15 Clive Hart, *Structure and Motif in "Finnegans Wake"* (London: Faber and Faber 1962), ch. 3.

16 Donald F. Theall, "Sendance of Sundance," 3.
17 Karl Marx, *The Economic and Philosophic Manuscripts of 1844*, trans. Martin Milligan (New York: International Publishers 1964), 140–1.
18 I have analyzed this passage in some detail elsewhere. See Donald F. Theall, *The Medium is the Rear View Mirror: Understanding McLuhan* (Montreal: McGill-Queen's Press 1971), 216–19, 245.
19 Gilles Deleuze, *Proust and Signs*, trans. Richard Howard (New York: George Braziller 1972), 149.

DAVID BRAYBROOKE

Academic Tenure in the Perspectives of Competition and Collegiality

How deep do the arguments about tenure as a university policy run? And do the arguments depend so much on imponderables, obvious and deep, that the issue cannot be resolved?

The adversaries of tenure cite neglect of duties to students by people whom the protection of tenure leaves virtually unaccountable to students or to anyone else, or neglect of research.[1] Both charges imply directly that the universities fall short in these instances of adequate performance in the pursuit of their chief objectives. But both charges root deeply in considerations of justice: Should people have pay and privileges protected by tenure and not deliver the services expected in return, or not deliver them copiously, as other people might who are shut out of the jobs? The advocates of tenure get down to principles perhaps even more quickly by portraying tenure as a defence of free inquiry and free expression, which are generally agreed to be matters of right involving both justice and the general welfare.[2] Some advocates make a humbler point:[3] that it is reasonable enough to give something like the same job security to academics as people in many other employments have, especially given the lifetime commitment expected to specializations (not just Egyptology; ornithology as well, and economic history) often hardly marketable outside universities. But even this humbler argument implies deep principles - justice again; the extent to which the market should be allowed to govern the character of employment.

Pressed just to the point of invoking these principles, however, the arguments do not run as deep everywhere as they could - and should. They do not run deep enough to settle the issue about tenure unless they lead to comparisons in depth, considering not just how far tenure conflicts with the principles or answers to them, but also whether there are alternative devices that answer to them better. Some adversaries of tenure recommend a system of renewable contracts under safeguards in Canadian legislation about human rights and in (they say) the changed climate in Canadian universities rendering tenure obsolete.[4] The advocates of tenure have replied that to let academic employment depend on the renewal of contracts is to shift the burden of proof, when vital questions of academic freedom do arise, from the authorities to the individual professor.[5] How can this help but put academic freedom at a disadvantage? Advocates may add that either the authorities will have a much larger measure of arbitrary discretion under the system of contracts than they do under the system of tenure, where they have to prove professional inadequacy to revoke tenure; or they will be so confined by other procedures, inside the universities or in the courts, as to make it at least as difficult to eject inadequate professors as it is under tenure.

That does not finish the comparison of tenure with alternative devices. There is no way of finishing it, even to the extent of having probable grounds for choosing between the system of tenure and the system of renewable contracts as a superior policy, without going more thoroughly into the costs and benefits at stake, and hence deepening the comparison both in detail and in respect to principles. In these respects and in others, the issue presents difficulties commonly encountered in policy-making: People cry up benefits without mentioning costs; cry down costs without mentioning benefits; bring both costs and benefits forward in the perspective of ideals or models imperfectly understood and certainly imperfectly explicit – in this case a model of competition transferred from the market-place versus a model of collegiality. Moreover, the information about the costs and benefits is not precise, or even (another matter) determinate enough to point one way rather than another.

The information is going to remain inadequate. We might have been lucky enough to have had consecutive experiments with the two systems in the same circumstances with the same people; but that is hardly the present case, and even if it were, the champions of the one or the other could always argue, as the champions of laissez-faire perennially argue, that the experiment had been interfered with too soon. We are not going to be able to count up utilities and disutilities and get a net utility (or disutility) figure on either side; that is a philosophical fantasy. Nor shall we be able in this case to cast up accounts in dollars and cents. Saving money on the input or supply side is not necessarily in question; people can be fierce adversaries of tenure without implying that fewer professors will be employed, or that professors' salaries will be reduced. On the output side, important aspects of output cannot be quantified: What is the dollar value, for example, of acquiring a taste for classical literature, or a capacity to assess statistical arguments?

Nevertheless we can proceed, proceeding with the issue about tenure as we proceed with other decisions under uncertainty. We not only often succeed – an everyday miracle – in coping with the uncertainty; on reflection we can recognize how we contrive to do so. We start where we are, with present institutions and the familiar, though incomplete, and often uncritically received, facts about their costs and benefits. We list the putative benefits of the alternative system and ask how convincing are the grounds for believing that they will be forthcoming? How far will they be offset by costs that we can identify with some probability beforehand? Then we match, feature by feature, the costs and benefits of the alternative system with the costs and benefits of the present one. Finally, if we are duly cautious, we recommend a change only if enough net benefits are probable to make the trouble of changing worthwhile. Even so, we recommend beginning by the smallest step that looks probably effective, or (perhaps more ambitiously) the smallest step consistent with our being able to pull back and mend matters if our expectations as to benefits meet disappointment.[6]

On this approach, we shall, we should, be cautious about giving up the benefits of the present system until we have made sure that the costs of it cannot be made tolerable. The present costs may themselves turn out to be tolerable once what is at stake with the system has been more fully appreciated. This needs to be seen for comparison with any alternative device; but I shall persevere with the comparison between tenure and the system of renewable contracts safeguarded by the courts and otherwise. There are questions about this system that will take us deep into what is at stake in any comparison – no deeper than justice, perhaps, but to a depth elsewhere that needs to be plumbed and brought into the comparison in a connected way even when justice has certified as passable all the devices in view. At that depth an ideal of university life – which extends to an ideal of what universities do for the general welfare – comes into view; and at that depth we shall be able to appreciate how delicately we must handle the question of accountability, under tenure or otherwise, if we are not to sacrifice more of the ideal than we are sacrificing already.

Nor shall we have to forfeit much in the generality of our argument by concentrating on the system of renewable contracts. Not only shall we be illustrating a general method of dealing with policy evaluation and decision-making under uncertainty. We shall also, by posing the issue on a continuum between the model of market competition perfected at one pole and the model of collegiality perfected at the other, reach results that bear upon more radical proposals. At any rate, since we shall be facing this way, and not considering how in the other direction more could be made of collegiality than tenure makes of it, our conclusions will hold for proposals that would go further toward the market ideal than renewable contracts of relatively long duration – three to six years – which I shall assume to be standard features of the system of contracts.[7] Few, even among the adversaries of tenure, would want to change to annual contracts; no one has to my knowledge suggested semester contracts or quarterly ones, much less daily hiring (though even daily hiring would not remove all the rigidities assumed away in the perfect markets of economic theory). I shall also assume that the test for renewing contracts would be adequate performance by the professors at present employed, not (closer to the market ideal) winning a new contract in a competition open to all comers.[8]

The adversaries of tenure who recommend the system of renewable contracts instead expect that, given the safeguards which they cite, decisions about renewal will turn on evidence of proficiency alone.[9] Furthermore, they reason that if failure to demonstrate proficiency at the times of contract renewal will lead to the loss of their jobs, professors will make sure (if they can) of demonstrating proficiency throughout their service, among other ways, by producing more published research that meets current professional standards. I think this expectation of more published research is a very probable empirical hypothesis. By generating more fear than the system of tenure does, the system of renewable contracts will incite some professors, who under tenure as it now operates do little or no research, to publish more frequently; and even incite some who do a substantial amount already to publish more, by way of precaution. I do not think anyone knows how large the effect would be. There are, everyone agrees, some professors who publish little or no research; but the adversaries of tenure typically do not supply any evidence to establish how many.[10] Nor do they consider carefully enough unpublished contributions. Socrates published nothing; Wittgenstein, in his lifetime, only a paper or two after publishing early in life his doctoral dissertation; Lord Acton, the historian, was seldom found in print. Moreover, there are contributions to consider besides contributions to research: teaching, of course; administrative leadership; leadership in professional organizations; community service. As the advocates of tenure incline to think, the professors who do no more than just get by under the system of tenure may form so small a proportion of the tenured professoriat as not to be worth the pain and trouble of holding them more strictly to account. My own estimate is that they form at most a proportion somewhere between 1 in 15 and 1 in 5.[11] (They are, even under the current system, held accountable in various ways and subjected to various penalties: They commonly must turn in to the dean an annual report of their activity. They suffer embarrassment in this connection. They are passed over for promotion; they are denied leave fellowships; they get no plums in visiting appointments; they lose respect and reputation; they forfeit honours.)

Let us assume, however, that the effect in more frequent publication of the system of renewable contracts would be a dramatic difference. Would more research in this sense, even if (as assumed) it meets current professional standards, be better research? There are at least two reasons for thinking that it would not be. One has to do with the difference between research activity and frequency of publication. Take two professors in the same field, equally industrious and equally proficient by current standards. One may publish very frequently, perhaps because he feels a childish delight in seeing his very own word-strings in print, perhaps because he thinks (realistically enough) that quantity will always count heavily with chairpersons, deans, committees, and other people passing judgment upon him. He may be ready to publish anything that a reputable journal or publishing house deems worth putting into print. His colleague may be more of a perfectionist, unwilling to let a work out of her hands until it has been revised and polished so that it is not merely arguably useful, but new and deep and thoroughly articulated in every particular. I myself have perhaps kept closer to the first professor's path than to the second's. But I would ask, does it advance research to frighten the second one into publishing more frequently?

The other reason for thinking that more research under the system of renewable contracts would not be better research lies in the practical impossibility of judging proficiency, including proficiency in research, by current professional standards, without running some danger of violating academic freedom. Political – ideological – considerations inevitably infect current professional standards, most blatantly in the social sciences, but not only there. Even if they did not, the history of science as currently understood, the history of art, the history of medicine, the history of literary criticism – the history of every academic subject –

teaches us that important new ideas and methods often have to fight their way to acceptance against an orthodoxy that believes with all sincerity that the ideas and methods violate elementary professional standards.[12] This is so, ironically, even when the orthodoxy means to put a premium on innovation, and to some degree, in some directions, actually does so.[13] Acting with all sincerity to uphold "elementary professional standards," people with established reputations in established positions will do their utmost on occasion to prevent the bearers of the new ideas and methods from having their contracts renewed. The occasions for renewing contracts will thus become so many opportunities to cut off unsettling new research whenever it begins. But will it begin, when the researchers know that it is so much safer for them to make only acceptable innovations and to avoid unsettling research?

It may be objected that established professors act on occasion with the same suppressive intentions when they make decisions about granting tenure. That is no doubt true.[14] In this respect the system of tenure makes a contribution, along with bureaucratic procedures for awarding research grants and the refereeing practices of the professional journals, to discouraging unsettling research. However, the contribution is a relatively small one, compared with the contribution that may be expected from the system of renewable contracts. Decisions about granting tenure come relatively early in a professor's career, early enough, one may hope, in most cases for ambitions of innovation to survive, and early enough to leave plenty of time and energy to carry innovations out. The implication that the candidates will have to bide their time through a probationary period in which they demonstrate their ability to meet conventional standards of proficiency will properly cause some anxiety about fields – like pure mathematics or theoretical physics – where grand innovations are produced by very young people. Special provisions, which would be as much departures from the system of renewable contracts as they would be from the current system of tenure, may have to operate in such fields. In most academic fields, however, it will perhaps be agreed that we may reasonably ask professors to demonstrate their ability by current tests before they embark (if they wish to embark) on careers of innovation. That agreement does not imply that they should be held to current standards of proficiency unremittingly, in the sense of being exposed repeatedly to reprisals by researchers of other orientations.

Adversaries of tenure look to the system of renewable contracts for substantial benefits in teaching as well as in research.[15] They are even more likely to be disappointed in this connection. The system may encourage a modest wave of innovations by impelling some professors to revise their approach to teaching; they will want to make sure of being effective enough to escape complaints. But the professors will not need to repeat these innovations, once their effectiveness has been established. Moreover, it would defeat the purpose of the innovations to do anything daring; for example, to go beyond the current norm in challenging students to work harder and learn more. The innovations will take place within the narrow range of conventionally safe methods. Worse, people who now, under the protection of tenure, feel free to undertake risky experiments (interdisciplinary programs; or, again, simply being more exacting than most of their colleagues) will have grounds – safety first – for abandoning such experiments.

The main drawbacks for teaching do not lie here, however. They lie in the effects of driving more time and energy into research. Where will the time and energy come from, if not in large part from teaching? The precautions that professors will take to make sure of meeting standards at the times of contract renewal will apply much more energetically to research than to teaching. Research will go on counting for more than teaching. It will count for more partly because scholars and scientists – even if they are themselves quite interested in teaching and committed to teaching well – value research more. That is why they are in the academic profession; they teach in return for being able to pursue their own studies rather than teach for its own sake. Research will go on counting for more than teaching also because the evidence respecting teaching is so indeterminate that professors who have reason to think their own teaching efforts less than acceptable may well discount the chances of their ever being unambiguously found out in this regard. Even if they are, they can hope to save themselves by a stronger record of specialized publication. As a result, the change in systems may lead to an unqualified reduction in teaching efforts: Professors who are doing a more than adequate job of teaching now will be frightened into reducing the attention that they are giving students in favour of putting more time and energy into research, while professors who are doing a less than adequate job do no more. If they are frightened into working harder, they work harder only in research.

Would this result be avoided by putting into effect much more thorough and regular methods of evaluating teaching than are now employed? Perfecting and administering such methods would require substantial human resources; one may wonder whether they could be found without diverting them from present commitments to research, or to teaching; but suppose they could. Even so I think the adversaries of tenure would find the result disappointing. With such methods, we could make sure that every professor met a minimum standard of effective teaching, and have this treated, like the minimum standard of research, as a necessary condition of having his contract renewed. Some professors who are running below that standard of teaching will revise their habits to meet it, and to that extent there will be an improvement in teaching. But there will be another effect, running in the opposite direction. While no professor who now meets the standard is likely to let herself fall below it, some professors who now more than meet it will cut back teaching in order to have more time and energy to meet the raised standards for research. That will still be the standard to which they must expect more importance to be attached. Moreover, that is the standard that will count, rather than teaching, if a professor loses out at his present university and has to seek an appointment elsewhere. Safety first implies as much mobility as he can contrive. Even thorough methods of evaluating teaching will depend (like grades for students) so much on local conditions that they will not furnish evidence easily transferable to other universities. A record of specialized publication, by contrast, transfers without discount. A department that needs a paleobotanist or an expert on Egyptian history during the Middle Kingdom is not going to worry unduly about evidence that the specialist in question has done no more in teaching than meet the minimum standard at her present university. They are not going to credit her for efforts in interdisciplinary programs, risky because they draw time and energy away from specialized publication; or for efforts, in some subjects almost as distracting, to bring her current research into play in her classes, and so make more of the shockingly unexploited possibilities of interanimation between research and teaching.

One may apprehend, therefore, from the system of contracts a net result amounting on the whole to worse teaching, in addition to a net result in research that raises frequency at the expense of quality and innovation. But these are not the worst things to be apprehended from changing to the system of contracts from the present system of tenure. At any rate they are evils that cannot be fully weighed if deeper effects of the system of contracts are not taken into account. I have two in mind, both of which imply sacrificing an ideal of university life and activity. One is the extinction of the sense of freedom conferred under the present system of gaining tenure after surmounting the tests of the probationary period. The other is the impairment to something that I shall call "collegiality," hoping to help restore to that notion the respect due it.[16]

Both the sense of freedom and the collegiality figure in the ideal of university life as a life fostering a milieu – indeed, a social union of milieux – in which people pursue studies out of the desire for knowledge rather than under compulsion, and freely assist each other in this enterprise.[17] Though universities at present – already too competitive, especially in research – make deplorably little of the opportunity, ideally students too would be enlisted in the milieu, kept abreast, for example, of the research going on in their major departments, and given some part in it as data-collectors, record-keepers, discussants, questioners. At times, and at their best, the fellowships of the colleges in the ancient English universities have perhaps achieved approximations of mutual aid in learning and of such a milieu; individual departments in other universities sometimes come even closer to realizing the ideal. The members of such departments, and some of their students, continually follow each other's work and continually collaborate in it, not only in classes, in laboratories, on field trips, in colloquia, but on a variety of less organized occasions, day by day, week by week. As collaboration develops among them, and with collaboration friendship, they come to appreciate the diversity of one another's contributions and of one another's virtues. Some publish more frequently; some publish more perfectly. Some are quick; others are patient. Some are lucid and well-organized; some are subtle and sensitive – some have, in Pascal's words, "l'esprit de géométrie"; others, "l'esprit de finesse." Their joint effort draws on a rich variety of contributions.[18]

Would it be sensible, even in an ideal account, to suppose that mutual appreciation in the milieu will extend to tolerating wide divergencies from prevailing ideas and methods, and thus allow as much room as innovations may need to make their way? The mutual following and collaboration to which I have alluded will depend on shared assumptions that enable the members of the milieu to talk to one another fruitfully. Ideas and methods that run counter to these assumptions, and the persons who would bring them in, may not be welcome. The milieu will have an orthodoxy of its own, founded on these assumptions; and if these assumptions are those that currently prevail in university after university, achieving the ideal in the given milieu will not favour departures from them.

On the other hand, this effect, when it is felt to the extent of actually excluding innovating researchers, will be felt, under the system of tenure, once and for all in any professor's career, at the time of granting

tenure. I do not wish to underrate this difficulty. One may notwith-
standing hope – a hope to some degree justified by experience – that
not all milieux will apply orthodox assumptions to the work of candidates. Some milieux may act conscientiously on a commitment to variety and self-criticism.[19] In some milieux the prevailing assumptions may
be unorthodox by the standards of the world at large. Moreover, even in
the most orthodox milieux, if tenure is granted early enough, innova-
tors will creep in.

Here the sense of freedom comes into play. Being granted tenure, in a
milieu of the sort or approximating the sort of which I have given an
ideal account, amounts to being recognized once and for all as a full
member of the *collegium*, with a vocation for joining in its work. It is like
being adopted by a family; becoming a full-fledged member of a monas-
tic order; taking one's place in the adult band of warriors, or in a knight-
ly order. I daresay these are very imperfect analogies; but they all have
in common the implication that one is no longer being scrutinized for
eligibility. In the academic case at least, this implication not only re-
moves anxiety about measuring up; it encourages one to choose one's
own topics of research and one's own ideas and methods in treating
them – not what other people are commited to, but what by one's own
notions promise to work best. An opportunity for innovation thus
arises; and some will be creative enough to seize it.

The innovations may disconcert the other members of the milieu. But
under the system of tenure there is little that they can do about it. In a
milieu such as I have described there is little that they will want to do
about it. Collegiality will induce a certain amount of sympathy with
any colleague's undertakings, including deviations. At the very least,
collegiality will restrain people from trying to eject a colleague even
when her undertakings seem bizarre. There was an international chess-
champion reputed to be so ruthless that he "fired" his mother when
she ceased to suit him. But happy families are not like that; nor are
happy monasteries; happy orders of knighthood; happy departments
in happy universities. Their happiness (and their success) lies in mutual
tolerance within the limits of mutual understanding about their joint
purposes and in making the most of a diversity of contributions – so
long as contributions are forthcoming.

The system of tenure assists collegiality by getting each person who
is granted tenure off to a good start as a member of the milieu, with the
respect of her colleagues based upon proof of her vocation and proficiency. The milieu, moreover, insofar as it approaches the ideal of collegiality, will strongly encourage her to retain that respect by vigorous

continuing activity. On the other hand, the system also puts some strains on collegiality, among them the strain incurred during decisions about granting tenure. If a department divides on this question in a particular instance, relations among the established members of the department, some favouring the candidate, some disfavouring him, may be stretched to the breaking point. Relations between established members, when they oppose tenure, and the candidate will deteriorate even farther. Are they not proposing to eject him from the *collegium*?

A generation ago departments may all too often have avoided these strains by giving tenure easily. Nowadays, when it is common to have faculty-wide committees review tenure decisions, departments behave more scrupulously; but now, given the intense competition for probationary appointments, strains occur infrequently because most candidates for tenure have strong cases. Yet I have some informal evidence from events during the transition to more rigorous decisions (when I fought for more rigour) and from current decisions denying promotion, that milieux which foster both a sense of freedom, including freedom to innovate, and collegiality can survive the strains. That such milieux could survive under a system of renewable contracts seems to me very doubtful. The system would at the very least multiply the strains; raise the level of anxiety; engender mutual fear throughout people's careers; increase the number of occasions on which members of the milieux fall bitterly at odds with each other. Under these multiplied strains would not the sense of freedom and the collegiality vanish? Each milieu would split up into so many atomic personal enterprises continually competing for advantage in the job market. This, of course, is just what some adversaries of tenure think they want. But are they sufficiently mindful of the drawbacks of turning all social institutions over to the regime of the market? Academic life is already very competitive. Are they sufficiently mindful of the incongruity, considering what universities should aim to be doing, of intensifying the competition, of converting universities into market-places, indeed of substituting miniature market-places for the *collegia* achieved here and there amid present difficulties.

One may still wonder whether the current system of tenure is not too comfortable, in the sense of being too easy to abuse – or at least of having been, in a cosier past, too easy to abuse. My estimates that the abuses inherited from past decisions to grant tenure run no higher than somewhere between 1 in 5 and 1 in 15 cases stand against thinking the abuses are enormous. There are in principle provisions for rectifying them. Tenure can be taken away after due process for gross neglect of duties whether in research or teaching. There are provisions short of revoking tenure for checking the abuses, like withholding promotion, or withholding what at some universities is called a Career Development Increment.

To the chagrin of advocates of tenure as well as of its adversaries, everyone involved – colleagues, chairpersons, deans – incline to shrink from the pain and trouble of using these provisions, and of course to shrink even more from the pain and trouble of revoking tenure.[20] Perhaps they are justified, more often than not, if they shrink. Not only will the gains in effective research and teaching not offset the losses in collegiality and other respects; they may forfeit their own effectiveness as participants in the *collegia*. There are people whom the very thought that others, somewhere, somehow, are free riding, excites beyond measure. They are ready to destroy family life in poor households if that is what it costs to make sure that there are no able-bodied adult males present in them who might benefit from aid to dependent children. No doubt they are ready to destroy collegiality and other good things in order to make sure that no professor anywhere is abusing tenure. Do we really want deans, chairpersons, or colleagues to act in this spirit?

Yet I expect the present system of tenure could stand a little more strain, and give improved results under it. We have at many universities a practice of periodically reviewing the performance of each individual department, employing for this purpose committees drawn from other departments in the same university with an external member or advisor drawn from the same subject at another university. Their collegiality is not nearly as much at risk in unfavourable recommendations as the collegiality of members of the same department, of the chairperson, of the dean. Might not such committees be asked to assess the performance of each member of the departments under review, with the power to recommend that Career Development Increments or their equivalent be withheld for the next several years in the case of a member who was not performing adequately in research or in teaching? The committee already has to read the c.v.'s of the professors in question; and should be able to spot flagrant deficiencies (which is all that in justice to the professors should be asked of the committee).

To forestall creating undue trouble for regular grievance procedures, the committee's judgment might be subject to appeal only to the faculty tenure committee (as being most abreast, in another connection, with current standards of proficiency).[21] It might be left to the next review committee to decide whether the increments should be restored or begin again – perhaps just left until the next review comittee decides, on the basis of the professor's performance then, that whether or not increments had been withheld in the past, there were no grounds for doing so now. Or, before the next review, but not before two or three years have elapsed, the department might recommend that the increments begin again; or be restored. A range of procedures offer themselves, none of them so much or so directly involving the department as to clash painfully with collegiality. Advocates of tenure might join adversaries of tenure in supporting experiments with some procedures in the range.

At bottom, the trouble with tenure may come not so much from tenure itself as from its combination with other social practices, chief among them the practice of committing everyone – not professors alone – to one career for each lifetime. A practice that allowed people who, through no moral failing do not bring at age 40 or age 50 the same zeal that they brought at age 30 to the history of the Middle Kingdom, to shift without great economic sacrifice to a career outside universities may be the most effective measure for sweeping university reform available to us. Tenure would still be needed to protect the unorthodox; but the trouble with it would substantially diminish.

There are grounds for generalizing this practice, and with it provisions for sabbatical re-education, to the whole work-force, increasing effectiveness and productivity wherever the practice reaches. Nor would generalizing it cost utopian amounts of funding. An American study estimates that a generalized practice of this kind for the whole American workforce would cost no more than 1.6 per cent of the United States GNP.[22] The same study reports from a survey that urban university professors much more than people in other vocations would choose to follow the same careers if they had to begin again.[23] Is this approach to happiness an unjust privilege? Are the collegial milieux that professors construct for themselves (when they do) too enjoyable to be deserved?

I am sure that professors do not deserve to be happy more than anyone else. But is it a sensible approach in social policy to destroy their milieux? Would it not be more sensible to try to multiply such milieux elsewhere? Quite independently of any question of reforming universities, something like collegiality has been argued to be at the bottom of Japan's industrial productivity. The opposite – the alienation of workers and the bloody-mindedness of labour relations in the English-speaking countries especially – not only reduces (through absenteeism, alcoholism, indifference) productivity, but also obstructs sensible measures to obtain full employment without inflation.[24] Taking employment under market conditions as the model for employment in universities not only seems unwarranted; it seems radically perverse. We shall do better to take the universities, when they work well under the collegial ideal, as offering a model for conditions of employment to be achieved elsewhere.[25]

NOTES

1 Sue Wood (then a student), in "Tenure – do professors need lifetime job security," *University Affairs* 13, no. 4 (April 1972): 5–6, opposes tenure chiefly because of effects on teaching that she ascribes to it. David J. Bercuson, Robert Bothwell, and J.L. Granatstein, *The Great Brain Robbery* (Toronto: McClelland and Stewart 1984), are chiefly concerned with effects on research (see their chapter on tenure, pp. 85–107).

2 A.E. Malloch, "Tenure – safeguard not freehold," *University Affairs* 13, no. 4 (April 1972): 2.

3 D. Braybrooke, "Tenure – illusion and reality," *University Affairs* 13, no. 4 (April 1972): 3.

4 Two University of Waterloo professors, cited by Sue Wood in "Tenure – do professors need lifetime job security," referred to such safeguards upon renouncing tenure.

5 Cf. A.E. Malloch, "Tenure – safeguard not freehold"; also in his annual report on behalf of the Committee on Academic Freedom, *CAUT Bulletin* 21, no. 1 (October 1972): 6–8.

6 The most general theory of decision-making under imperfect information or uncertainty is Herbert A. Simon's and it sails under the name that he gave it of "satisficing." See his *Models of Man, Social and Rational* (New York: Wiley 1961), 61, 70–71; and other works, including *Reason in Human Affairs* (Stanford: Stanford University Press 1983). A related theory, "disjointed incrementalism," formulated specifically for application to social policy, and reflected in the brief sketch just given, can be found in D. Braybrooke and C.E. Lindblom, *A Strategy of Decision: Policy Evaluation as a Social Process* (New York: The Free Press 1963); in other writings by Lindblom, especially "Still Muddling, Not Yet Through," in *Public Administration Review* 39, no. 6 (November/December 1979): 517–26; and in D. Braybrooke, "Scale; Combination; Opposition – a Rethinking of Incrementalism," *Ethics* 95, no. 4 (July 1985): 920–33. The argument in these works concentrates, as the term "incrementalism" suggests, on the rationality of proceeding by small

steps. The matching process is most fully expounded in chapter 5 ("Utilitarianism without Utility") of D. Braybrooke, *Meeting Needs* (Princeton: Princeton University Press 1987).

7 Bercuson et al. suggest five-year contracts (saying nothing about how the change-over from tenure is to be managed without breaking faith with people who accepted jobs or continued in them because they were given tenure). *The Great Brain Robbery*, 105.

8 Leo Groarke, cited by Bercuson et al. without attention to this point, seems to have full open competition in mind. See Bercuson et al., *The Great Brain Robbery*, 100–1. Groarke's article itself ("Tenure as injustice," *CAUT Bulletin* 29, no. 1 [February 1982] 3–4) bears out the impression.

9 Wood, Bercuson et al., and Groarke, cited in previous notes, all expect this effect.

10 Bercuson et al., *The Great Brain Robbery*, assert, "Many of those who enjoy the perquisites of the university have long ago ceased doing anything to earn them" (85–6), for "if a faculty member with tenure meets his classes, marks his papers, and holds an occasional office hour, he is safe" (p. 98). They put no number to "many"; nor (what is much more significant) do they give any estimate of the proportion. There are many cases of food poisoning in Canada every year; that does not make most meals in Canada poisonous. In another passage, they take from the CAUT an estimate of 25 academics' having lost tenure in Canada during the 15 years prior to 1983. They comment, "There are now 33,000 academics employed in Canada's universities. Are there only twenty-five incompetents who have taught in the university system? ... The law of averages is still in force, we think, and to ask the question is to answer it." What are they thinking of as "the law of averages"? The notion of median travels in the same company as "average" (in the sense of mean) and is sometimes thought of as a kind of average. It is an a priori truth that on any measure, including a measure of competence, applied to academics, as many will fail at or below the median value as fall at or above it. Suppose we briskly dismissed all those who now rate at less than the median for competence. Should we then dismiss up to half of those who remain? They, too, will fall below the current median for competence. Alternatively, it has been suggested to me, we might suppose that Bercuson et al. simply mean that 25 out of 33,000 is a much lower figure than would be given for the year-in year-out mean figure for dismissals on the ground of incompetence in other occupations. But the figure 25 does not include people dismissed as not having gained tenure; or the number of people with tenure eased into administrative jobs or persuaded to resign. And would the number of lawyers who are ejected from partnerships run higher? Would

the number of physicians who lose hospital privileges, or their licenses? With the help of my research assistant Larry Swatuck I have made an effort to find answers to these questions. He tried to get figures for Nova Scotia; for Ontario; for Canada as a whole. The figures for Canada as a whole turned out to require more extensive inquiry than we had time for. The relevant medical authorities in Ontario have been much less open and forthcoming than those in Nova Scotia. We had scattered, helpful responses from legal authorities in Ontario and several other provinces which came in too late to be reproduced here; they fall in with the responses obtained in Nova Scotia. In Nova Scotia the members of the bar numbered 903 in 1977 and 1302 in 1987; during that period *six* lawyers in Nova Scotia were disbarred. In 1977, there were 1408 doctors licensed to practise medicine in Nova Scotia as against 1747 in 1986. During that period *two* of them lost their licenses. Taking the mean between the earlier and later figures in each case as the base, the rate of disbarment was 0.005; of delicensing, 0.001. At the Nova Scotia rate for lawyers disbarred, 165 academics out of 33,000 would have lost tenure; at the Nova Scotia rate for physicians delicensed, 33 would have. But both these figures overstate the comparison, since they are based on the figure 33,000, the end of period figure not the base mean. Moreover, the lawyers' figure does not correspond to incompetence in any simple way, but to temptations that rarely come the way of academics. How many lawyers are ejected from partnerships on grounds of incompetence? About as few, one might speculate, as stop practising on the same grounds.

11 I arrive at this figure by a process designed to make sure that it is overstated – maybe grossly overstated – rather than understated. I took the rosters of the departments of philosophy at every university in the Maritime Provinces for which a roster is given in the *Commonwealth Universities Yearbook 1986* (London: Association of Commonwealth Universities 1986), vol. 2, that is to say, every such university that has a separate department of philosophy, namely 10, except Moncton. Then, drawing on my own knowledge (quite intimate without being complete) of activity in these departments, I classified the professors on the rosters under three headings: (1) doing as little as safety requires (the criterion invoked by Bercuson et al. in their denunciations – see the previous note); (2) active enough in discussions, conferences, and publications to keep up with their field; (3) preparing and publishing books and articles subject to rigorous editorial and refereeing procedures. I took no account of contributions other than to research; they may be – in some cases I know they are – considerable for people put under (2), or even under (1). When, in spite of my long acquaintance with philosophical activity in the Maritimes, I did not

know anything about people named on the rosters (I expect, in most cases, newcomers), I assigned them in equal numbers, department by department, to headings (1) and (2), except that when there was an odd number (1 or more), I assigned 1 more to (1). Taking the rosters as a whole, without trying to separate out tenured professors, I found 9 at level (1), 26 at level (2), and 12 at level (3), or 38 running above the level denounced by Bercuson et al., where 19% of the total number fell. I also computed figures for various subgroups of the total roster population: Associate Professors and Professors, as an approximation to the subgroup with tenure; people above the rank of Lecturer known to me – another approximation; Associate Professors and Professors, omitting Professors within 4 years of retirement (assuming retirement at 65; they would not be policed any more closely under the system of renewable contracts than they are under the system of tenure). In these three subgroups, the numbers falling under (1), (2), and (3) are respectively, 7, 23, 10 (17½% at the minimal activity level); 3, 22, 12 (8% at the minimal activity level). The highest proportion at the minimal activity level is about 1 in 5; the lowest, a bit lower than 1 in 12. Is philosophy different from other subjects? It does not seem to be different in this connection from political science. I do not know as much about so many departments of political science in the Maritime Provinces as I do about departments of philosophy. However, I made the same four comparisons for the three departments of political science that I know best and the figures come out: 2, 11, 17; 1, 6, 17; 0, 10, 17; 1, 6, 11. These figures are heavily influenced by one department, where the figures for the first comparison are 0, 4, 15, the top of the range. It is the one department of political science in the region that has a substantial graduate program extending to the PHD. The department of philosophy at the same university is unique in the region in that respect, too, and places at the top of the range for philosophy: 0, 2, 11. These departments are probably much more like typical departments elsewhere in Canada. About half the Canadian universities outside the Maritimes have PHD. programs in philosophy, as against 1 in 11 in the Maritimes. What shall we take as a conservative estimate for the better end of the range conservatively hypothesized for the proportion of professors in category (1) in departments of philosophy or political science or other subjects across Canada? I take 1 in 15, the worst figure in the comparisons that I have made for three Maritime departments of political science. But if carrying on PHD. programs has the association with professors' activity that I conjecture it has, 1 in 15 may well overstate the proportion.

12 The opposition descending to persecution that Galileo, Semmelweis, and Leavis met with is all too likely to be typical even now, given the account

of scientific activity that historians of science like Thomas S. Kuhn have made prevailing. Science, according to Kuhn, works normally under a received paradigm shared by the relevant scientific community. "Recognition of the existence of a uniquely competent professional group and acceptance of its role as the exclusive arbiter of professional achievements" implies that "the group's members, as individuals and by virtue of their shared training and experience must be seen as the sole possessors of the rules of the game or of some equivalent basis for unequivocal judgments. To doubt that they shared some basis for evaluations would be to admit the existence of incompatible standards of scientific achievement" (Kuhn, *The Structure of Scientific Revolutions*, 2d ed., [Chicago: University of Chicago Press 1970], 168). Kuhn quotes Max Planck, remarking in his autobiography, "A new scientific truth does not triumph by convincing its opponents and making them see the light, but rather because its opponents eventually die, and a new generation grows up that is familiar with it" (Kuhn, 151). All this is in a field where the facts are harder and the commitment to precise empirical tests firmer than elsewhere. The history of science is closer to the history of art than most scientists might wish to acknowledge; and the history of art, though not the history of a university subject, gives us a useful repeated illustration of the opposition of "academic" values to innovation. In a footnote, Kuhn cites the case of Lord Rayleigh, submitting to the British Association – "after his reputation was established" – "a paper on some paradoxes of electrodynamics. His name was inadvertently omitted when the paper was first sent, and the paper itself was at first refused as the work of some 'paradoxer.' Shortly afterwards, with the author's name in place, the paper was accepted with profuse apologies" (Kuhn, *The Structure of Scientific Revolutions*, 153, footnote). This incident illustrates simultaneously (1) the dangers of blind refereeing; (2) the opposition of the establishment to innovations; (3) the freedom that an established figure can enjoy once established.

13 Unlike Galileo's opponents, no one nowadays in any field would admit to acting to suppress new ideas and methods. Moreover, the sciences have to some extent institutionalized innovation. But on Kuhn's showing the firmest institutionalization presupposes a paradigm in theory and methods and favours innovations within the limits of that paradigm. It is hard to see how radical innovations could be provided for institutionally in anything like the same way without sacrificing the benefits of "normal science" – science for Kuhn as it characteristically works, exploiting a paradigm and sacrificing with normal science the characteristic way in which a revolution is prepared (Kuhn, *The Structure of Scientific Revolutions*, 52, 65).

14 It is just this point that worried A.E. Malloch in "Academic Freedom and the Canadian Professor: Part II," *CAUT Bulletin* 30, no. 1 (February 1983): 11–14.

15 See especially Sue Wood, "Tenure – do professors need lifetime job security."

16 Opponents of unionization have charged that unionizing college faculties would destroy collegiality – between them and faculty members favouring unions; between those members and deans, vice-presidents, presidents, et al. In my experience, neither effect has come about; and "collegiality" is too good an idea for its name to be used simply as an anti-union slogan.

17 For the idea of a "social union" (mutual aid with a division of labour), see John Rawls, *A Theory of Justice* (Cambridge, MA: Harvard University Press 1970), 523ff. Each milieu (here, basically, a university department, perhaps sometimes a circle in which several departments intersect) that I am referring to, would itself be a social union. A social union of milieux (in the present case, a university) would be what Rawls calls "a social union of social unions" (p. 527).

18 An even more famous authority connects variety of contributions with the spirit of community: "Now there are diversities of gifts, but the same Spirit. And there are differences of administrations, but the same Lord. And there are diversities of operations, but it is the same God which worketh all in all ... to one is given by the spirit the word of wisdom; to another the word of knowledge by the same Spirit; to another faith by the same Spirit; to another the gifts of healing by the same Spirit; to another the working of miracles; to another prophecy; to another discerning of spirits; to another divers kinds of tongues; to another the interpretation of tongues; but all these worketh that one and the self-same Spirit, dividing to every man severally as he will" 1 Corinthians 12:4–11.

19 The term "self-criticism" comes from A.E. Malloch, "Academic Freedom and the Canadian Professor: Part II." Malloch says there in addition: "The academic profession is profoundly committed to a continual recreation of itself. To honour that commitment, the profession must be prepared to extend to its own members a freedom which at times may seem to bring the profession to the edge of anarchy" (14).

20 Malloch again, "Academic Freedom and the Canadian Professor"; also in his *University Affairs* article "Tenure – safeguard not freedom."

21 The model for this suggestion is the feature of tenure-granting procedures at some universities providing for appeal only, outside the regular grievance procedures, to a special panel.

22 *Work in America*, Report of a Special Task Force to the Secretary of Health,

Education, and Welfare (Cambridge, MA: The MIT Press 1973), 129, 131. I
am assuming, where the book assumes that only half of the workers
would take up the sabbaticals to be offered them (six months every seven
years, or one year every fourteen), that all would accept. Giving the whole
work-force sabbaticals as generous in frequency as academic ones would
presumably cost little more than 3% of GNP.

23 *Work in America*, 16. I do not know about rural university professors.

24 On "job-related pathologies," see *Work in America*, 28, 81–90. On the ob-
struction to an incomes policy that might give full employment without
inflation, see John Cornwall, *The Conditions for Economic Recovery* (Oxford:
Martin Robertson 1983), chap. 12.

25 I wish to thank my prime, first-hand example of a collegial milieu – the
Department of Philosophy at Dalhousie, professors and students, for listening to a preliminary version of this paper and responding to it; and
thank, too, my colleague in the Dalhousie Department of Political Science,
Herman Bakvis, for giving me good advice about the statistical notes, in
which I have not, alas! been in a position to make the most of the advice.

Contributors

ELAINE BANDER is a member of the English Department of Dawson College (Montreal). Her interest in Jane Austen began with her doctoral thesis, done under the supervision of A.E. Malloch. She has published articles on Austen and on aspects of detective fiction.

MAGGIE BERG is a member of the Department of English at Queen's University. She is the author of *Jane Eyre: Portrait of a Life* (Boston: G.K. Hall 1987).

DAVID BRAYBROOKE is professor of Philosophy and Political Science at Dalhousie University. His many philosophical works include *Three Tests for Democracy: Personal Rights: Human Welfare: Collective Preference* (New York: Random House 1968) and most recently *Meeting Needs* (Princeton: Princeton University Press 1987).

CHARLES ABBOTT CONWAY is a member of the Department of English at McGill University where he teaches Old English. He is the author of *The Vita Christi of Ludolph of Saxony and Late Medieval Devotion Centred on the Incarnation* (Salzburg: James Hogg 1976).

LESLIE DUER is a member of the Department of English at McGill University where he teaches Elizabethan and Jacobean drama. He is presently at work on the problems of representation and narrative disclosure in the English Renaissance.

DEAN FRYE is a member of the Department of English at McGill University where he teaches Renaissance literature.

ALAN HEUSER is a member of the Department of English at McGill University. He is the author of *The Shaping Vision of Gerard Manley Hopkins* (London: Oxford University Press 1958) and *Selected Literary Criticism of Louis MacNeice* (Oxford: Clarendon Press 1987).

DAVID F. THEALL is university professor and past president of Trent University. He is the author of *The Medium is the Rear View Mirror* (Montreal and Kingston: McGill-Queen's University Press 1971).

GARY WIHL is a former student of A.E. Malloch and now teaches literary theory in the Department of English at McGill. He is the author of *Ruskin and the Rhetoric of Infallibility* (New Haven: Yale University Press 1985).

DAVID WILLIAMS is chairman of the Department of English at McGill University. He is the author of *Cain and Beowulf: A Study in Secular Allegory* (Toronto: University of Toronto Press 1982) and *Chaucer's Canterbury Tales: A Literary Pilgrimage* (Boston: G.K. Hall 1987).

Index

Sterne, Lawrence, 116
Swift, Jonathan, 116
Synge, J.M., 7

Tave, Stuart, 56
Taylor, Frederick Winslow, 119
Taylor, Thomas, 119
Thatcher, Margaret, 65
Trollope, Anthony, 47

Valéry, Paul, 111
Van Dyke, Sir Anthony, 34, 35, 37
Varro, 100–1

Vaulx, Dr James, 32–7 passim, 41, 42
Vaulx, Francis, 33
Veatch, Henry Babcock, 79–80, 91
Veronese, Paolo, 32
Vico, Giambattista, 112
Voltaire, 50

Watt, James, 115
Weaver, Harriet Shaw, 111
Webster, John, 34
Wisdom, Stephen(s?), 35
Wittgenstein, Ludwig, 130
Wright Brothers, 112